TABLE OF CONTENTS

Secret Key #1 - Time is Your Greatest Enemy

Pace Yourself

Wear a watch. At the beginning of the test, check the time (or start a chronometer on your watch to count the minutes), and check the time after every few questions to make sure you are "on schedule."

If you are forced to speed up, do it efficiently. Usually one or more answer choices can be eliminated without too much difficulty. Above all, don't panic. Don't speed up and just begin guessing at random choices. By pacing yourself, and continually monitoring your progress against your watch, you will always know exactly how far ahead or behind you are with your available time. If you find that you are one minute behind on the test, don't skip one question without spending any time on it, just to catch back up. Take 15 fewer seconds on the next four questions, and after four questions you'll have caught back up. Once you catch back up, you can continue working each problem at your normal pace.

Furthermore, don't dwell on the problems that you were rushed on. If a problem was taking up too much time and you made a hurried guess, it must be difficult. The difficult questions are the ones you are most likely to miss anyway, so it isn't a big loss. It is better to end with more time than you need than to run out of time.

Lastly, sometimes it is beneficial to slow down if you are constantly getting ahead of time. You are always more likely to catch a careless mistake by working more slowly than quickly, and among very high-scoring test takers (those who are likely to have lots of time left over), careless errors affect the score more than mastery of material.

Secret Key #2 - Guessing is not Guesswork

You probably know that guessing is a good idea - unlike other standardized tests, there is no penalty for getting a wrong answer. Even if you have no idea about a question, you still have a 20-25% chance of getting it right.

Most test takers do not understand the impact that proper guessing can have on their score. Unless you score extremely high, guessing will significantly contribute to your final score.

Monkeys Take the Test

What most test takers don't realize is that to insure that 20-25% chance, you have to guess randomly. If you put 20 monkeys in a room to take this test, assuming they answered once per question and behaved themselves, on average they would get 20-25% of the questions correct. Put 20 test takers in the room, and the average will be much lower among guessed questions. Why?

1. The test writers intentionally write deceptive answer choices that "look" right. A test taker has no idea about a question, so picks the "best looking" answer, which is often wrong. The monkey has no idea what looks good and what doesn't, so will consistently be lucky about 20-25% of the time.
2. Test takers will eliminate answer choices from the guessing pool based on a hunch or intuition. Simple but correct answers often

- 4 -

get excluded, leaving a 0% chance of being correct. The monkey has no clue, and often gets lucky with the best choice.

This is why the process of elimination endorsed by most test courses is flawed and detrimental to your performance- test takers don't guess, they make an ignorant stab in the dark that is usually worse than random.

$5 Challenge

Let me introduce one of the most valuable ideas of this course- the $5 challenge:

You only mark your "best guess" if you are willing to bet $5 on it.
You only eliminate choices from guessing if you are willing to bet $5 on it.

Why $5? Five dollars is an amount of money that is small yet not insignificant, and can really add up fast (20 questions could cost you $100). Likewise, each answer choice on one question of the test will have a small impact on your overall score, but it can really add up to a lot of points in the end.

The process of elimination IS valuable. The following shows your chance of guessing it right:

If you eliminate wrong answer choices until only this many remain:	Chance of getting it correct:
1	100%
2	50%
3	33%

However, if you accidentally eliminate the right answer or go on a hunch for an incorrect answer, your chances drop dramatically: to 0%. By guessing among all the answer choices, you are GUARANTEED to have a shot at the right

answer.

That's why the $5 test is so valuable- if you give up the advantage and safety of a pure guess, it had better be worth the risk.

What we still haven't covered is how to be sure that whatever guess you make is truly random. Here's the easiest way:

Always pick the first answer choice among those remaining.

Such a technique means that you have decided, **before you see a single test question**, exactly how you are going to guess- and since the order of choices tells you nothing about which one is correct, this guessing technique is perfectly random.

This section is not meant to scare you away from making educated guesses or eliminating choices- you just need to define when a choice is worth eliminating. The $5 test, along with a pre-defined random guessing strategy, is the best way to make sure you reap all of the benefits of guessing.

Secret Key #3 - Practice Smarter, Not Harder

Many test takers delay the test preparation process because they dread the awful amounts of practice time they think necessary to succeed on the test. We have refined an effective method that will take you only a fraction of the time.

There are a number of "obstacles" in your way to succeed. Among these are answering questions, finishing in time, and mastering test-taking strategies. All must be executed on the day of the test at peak performance, or your score will suffer. The test is a mental marathon that has a large impact on your future.

Just like a marathon runner, it is important to work your way up to the full challenge. So first you just worry about questions, and then time, and finally strategy:

Success Strategy

1. Find a good source for practice tests.
2. If you are willing to make a larger time investment, consider using more than one study guide- often the different approaches of multiple authors will help you "get" difficult concepts.
3. Take a practice test with no time constraints, with all study helps "open book." Take your time with questions and focus on applying strategies.
4. Take a practice test with time constraints, with all guides "open book."
5. Take a final practice test with no open material and time limits

If you have time to take more practice tests, just repeat step 5. By gradually exposing yourself to the full rigors of the test environment, you will condition your mind to the stress of test day and maximize your success.

Secret Key #4 - Prepare, Don't Procrastinate

Let me state an obvious fact: if you take the test three times, you will get three different scores. This is due to the way you feel on test day, the level of

preparedness you have, and, despite the test writers' claims to the contrary, some tests WILL be easier for you than others.

Since your future depends so much on your score, you should maximize your chances of success. In order to maximize the likelihood of success, you've got to prepare in advance. This means taking practice tests and spending time learning the information and test taking strategies you will need to succeed.

Never take the test as a "practice" test, expecting that you can just take it again if you need to. Feel free to take sample tests on your own, but when you go to take the official test, be prepared, be focused, and do your best the first time!

Secret Key #5 - Test Yourself

Everyone knows that time is money. There is no need to spend too much of your time or too little of your time preparing for the test. You should only spend as much of your precious time preparing as is necessary for you to get the score you need.

Once you have taken a practice test under real conditions of time constraints, then you will know if you are ready for the test or not.

If you have scored extremely high the first time that you take the practice test, then there is not much point in spending countless hours studying. You are already there.

Benchmark your abilities by retaking practice tests and seeing how much you have improved. Once you score high enough to guarantee success, then you are ready.

If you have scored well below where you need, then knuckle down and begin studying in earnest. Check your improvement regularly through the use of practice tests under real conditions. Above all, don't worry, panic, or give up. The key is perseverance!

Then, when you go to take the test, remain confident and remember how well you did on the practice tests. If you can score high enough on a practice test, then you can do the same on the real thing.

General Strategies

The most important thing you can do is to ignore your fears and jump into the test immediately- do not be overwhelmed by any strange-sounding terms. You have to jump into the test like jumping into a pool- all at once is the easiest way.

Make Predictions

As you read and understand the question, try to guess what the answer will be. Remember that several of the answer choices are wrong, and once you begin reading them, your mind will immediately become cluttered with answer choices designed to throw you off. Your mind is typically the most focused immediately after you have read the question and digested its contents. If you can, try to predict what the correct answer will be. You may be surprised at what you can predict.

Quickly scan the choices and see if your prediction is in the listed answer choices. If it is, then you can be quite confident that you have the right answer. It still won't hurt to check the other answer choices, but most of the time, you've got it!

Answer the Question

It may seem obvious to only pick answer choices that answer the question, but the test writers can create some excellent answer choices that are wrong. Don't pick an answer just because it sounds right, or you believe it to be true. It MUST answer the question. Once you've made your selection, always go back and check it against the question and make sure that you didn't misread the question, and the answer choice does answer the question posed.

Benchmark

After you read the first answer choice, decide if you think it sounds correct or not. If it doesn't, move on to the next answer choice. If it does, mentally mark that answer choice. This doesn't mean that you've definitely selected it as your answer choice, it just means that it's the best you've seen thus far. Go ahead and read the next choice. If the next choice is worse than the one you've already selected, keep going to the next answer choice. If the next choice is better than the choice you've already selected, mentally mark the new answer choice as your best guess.

The first answer choice that you select becomes your standard. Every other answer choice must be benchmarked against that standard. That choice is correct until proven otherwise by another answer choice beating it out. Once you've decided that no other answer choice seems as good, do one final check to ensure that your answer choice answers the question posed.

Valid Information

Don't discount any of the information provided in the question. Every piece of information may be necessary to determine the correct answer. None of the information in the question is there to throw you off (while the answer choices will certainly have information to throw you off). If two seemingly unrelated topics are discussed, don't ignore either. You can be confident there is a relationship, or it wouldn't be included in the question, and you are probably going to have to determine what is that relationship to find the answer.

Avoid "Fact Traps"

Don't get distracted by a choice that is factually true. Your search is for the answer that answers the question. Stay focused and don't fall for an answer that is true but incorrect. Always go back to the question and make sure you're choosing an answer that actually answers the question and is not just a true statement. An answer can be factually correct, but it MUST answer the question asked. Additionally, two answers can both be seemingly correct, so be sure to read all of the answer choices, and make sure that you get the one that BEST answers the question.

Milk the Question

Some of the questions may throw you completely off. They might deal with a subject you have not been exposed to, or one that you haven't reviewed in years. While your lack of knowledge about the subject will be a hindrance, the question itself can give you many clues that will help you find the correct answer. Read the question carefully and look for clues. Watch particularly for adjectives and nouns describing difficult terms or words that you don't recognize. Regardless of if you completely understand a word or not, replacing it with a synonym either provided or one you more familiar with may help you to understand what the questions are asking. Rather than wracking your mind about specific detailed information concerning a difficult term or word, try to use mental substitutes that are easier to understand.

The Trap of Familiarity

Don't just choose a word because you recognize it. On difficult questions, you may not recognize a number of words in the answer choices. The test writers don't put "make-believe" words on the test; so don't think that just because you only recognize all the words in one answer choice means that answer choice must be correct. If you only recognize words in one answer choice, then focus on that one. Is it correct? Try your best to determine if it is correct. If it is, that is great, but if it doesn't, eliminate it. Each word and answer choice you eliminate increases your chances of getting the question correct, even if you then have to guess among the unfamiliar choices.

Eliminate Answers

Eliminate choices as soon as you realize they are wrong. But be careful! Make sure you consider all of the possible answer choices. Just because one appears right, doesn't mean that the next one won't be even better! The test writers will usually put more than one good answer choice for every question, so read all of them. Don't worry if you are stuck between two that seem right. By getting down to just two remaining possible choices, your odds are now 50/50. Rather than wasting too much time, play the odds. You are guessing, but guessing wisely, because you've been able to knock out some of the answer choices that you know are wrong. If you are eliminating choices and realize that the last answer choice you are left with is also obviously wrong, don't panic. Start over and consider each choice again. There may easily be something that you missed the first time and will realize on the second pass.

Tough Questions

If you are stumped on a problem or it appears too hard or too difficult, don't waste time. Move on! Remember though, if you can quickly check for obviously incorrect answer choices, your chances of guessing correctly are greatly improved. Before you completely give up, at least try to knock out a couple of possible answers. Eliminate what you can and then guess at the remaining answer choices before moving on.

Brainstorm

If you get stuck on a difficult question, spend a few seconds quickly brainstorming. Run through the complete list of possible answer choices. Look at each choice and ask yourself, "Could this answer the question satisfactorily?" Go through each answer choice and consider it independently of the other. By systematically going through all possibilities, you may find something that you would otherwise overlook. Remember that when you get stuck, it's important to try to keep moving.

Read Carefully

Understand the problem. Read the question and answer choices carefully. Don't miss the question because you misread the terms. You have plenty of time to read each question thoroughly and make sure you understand what is being asked. Yet a happy medium must be attained, so don't waste too much time. You must read carefully, but efficiently.

Face Value

When in doubt, use common sense. Always accept the situation in the problem at face value. Don't read too much into it. These problems will not require you to make huge leaps of logic. The test writers aren't trying to throw you off with a cheap trick. If you have to go beyond creativity and make a leap of logic in order to have an answer choice answer the question, then you should look at the other answer choices. Don't overcomplicate the problem by creating theoretical relationships or explanations that will warp time or space. These are normal problems rooted in reality. It's just that the applicable relationship or explanation may not be readily apparent and you have to figure things out. Use your common sense to interpret anything that isn't clear.

Prefixes

If you're having trouble with a word in the question or answer choices, try dissecting it. Take advantage of every clue that the word might include. Prefixes and suffixes can be a huge help. Usually they allow you to determine a basic meaning. Pre- means before, post- means

after, pro - is positive, de- is negative. From these prefixes and suffixes, you can get an idea of the general meaning of the word and try to put it into context. Beware though of any traps. Just because con is the opposite of pro, doesn't necessarily mean congress is the opposite of progress!

Hedge Phrases

Watch out for critical "hedge" phrases, such as likely, may, can, will often, sometimes, often, almost, mostly, usually, generally, rarely, sometimes. Question writers insert these hedge phrases to cover every possibility. Often an answer choice will be wrong simply because it leaves no room for exception. Avoid answer choices that have definitive words like "exactly," and "always".

Switchback Words

Stay alert for "switchbacks". These are the words and phrases frequently used to alert you to shifts in thought. The most common switchback word is "but". Others include although, however, nevertheless, on the other hand, even though, while, in spite of, despite, regardless of.

New Information

Correct answer choices will rarely have completely new information included. Answer choices typically are straightforward reflections of the material asked about and will directly relate to the question. If a new piece of information is included in an answer choice that doesn't even seem to relate to the topic being asked about, then that answer choice is likely incorrect. All of the information needed to answer the question is usually provided for you, and so you should not have to make guesses that are unsupported or choose answer choices that require unknown information that cannot be reasoned on its own.

Time Management

On technical questions, don't get lost on the technical terms. Don't spend too much time on any one question. If you don't know what a term means, then since you don't have a dictionary, odds are you aren't going to get much further. You should immediately recognize terms as whether or not you know them. If you don't, work with the other clues that you have, the other answer choices and terms provided, but don't waste too much time trying to figure out a difficult term.

Contextual Clues

Look for contextual clues. An answer can be right but not correct. The contextual clues will help you find the answer that is most right and is correct. Understand the context in which a phrase or statement is made. This will help you make important distinctions.

Don't Panic

Panicking will not answer any questions for you. Therefore, it isn't helpful. When you first see the question, if your mind goes blank, take a deep breath. Force yourself to mechanically go through the steps of solving the problem and using the strategies you've learned.

Pace Yourself

Don't get clock fever. It's easy to be overwhelmed when you're looking at a page full of questions, your mind is full of random thoughts and feeling confused, and the clock is ticking down faster than you would like. Calm down and maintain the pace that you have set for yourself. As long as you are on track by monitoring your pace, you are guaranteed to have enough time for yourself. When you get to the last few minutes of the test, it may seem like you won't have enough time left, but if you only have as many questions as you should have left at that point, then you're right on track!

Answer Selection

The best way to pick an answer choice is to eliminate all of those that are wrong, until only one is left and confirm that is the correct answer. Sometimes though, an answer choice may immediately look right. Be careful! Take a second to make sure that the other choices are not equally obvious. Don't make a hasty mistake. There are only two times that you should stop before checking other answers. First is when you are positive that the answer choice you have selected is correct. Second is when time is almost out and you have to make a quick guess!

Check Your Work

Since you will probably not know every term listed and the answer to every question, it is important that you get credit for the ones that you do know. Don't miss any questions through careless mistakes. If at all possible, try to take a second to look back over your answer selection and make sure you've selected the correct answer choice and haven't made a costly careless mistake (such as marking an answer choice that you didn't mean to mark). This quick double check should more than pay for itself in caught mistakes for the time it costs.

Beware of Directly Quoted Answers

Sometimes an answer choice will repeat word for word a portion of the question or reference section. However, beware of such exact duplication – it may be a trap! More than likely, the correct choice will paraphrase or summarize a point, rather than being exactly the same wording.

Slang

Scientific sounding answers are better than slang ones. An answer choice that begins "To compare the outcomes..." is much more likely to be correct than one that begins "Because some people insisted…"

Extreme Statements

Avoid wild answers that throw out highly controversial ideas that are proclaimed as established fact. An answer choice that states the "process should used in certain situations, if…" is much more likely to be correct than one that states the "process should be discontinued completely." The first is a calm rational statement and doesn't even make a definitive, uncompromising stance, using a hedge word "if" to provide wiggle room, whereas the second choice is a radical idea and far more extreme.

Answer Choice Families

When you have two or more answer choices that are direct opposites or parallels, one of them is usually the correct answer. For instance, if one answer choice states "x increases" and another answer choice states "x decreases" or "y increases," then those two or three answer choices are very similar in construction and fall into the same family of answer choices. A family of answer choices is when two or three answer choices are very similar in construction, and yet often have a directly opposite meaning. Usually the correct answer choice will be in that family of answer choices. The "odd man out" or answer choice that doesn't seem to fit the parallel construction of the other answer choices is more likely to be incorrect

Top 20 Test Taking Tips

1. Carefully follow all the test registration procedures
2. Know the test directions, duration, topics, question types, how many questions
3. Setup a flexible study schedule at least 3-4 weeks before test day
4. Study during the time of day you are most alert, relaxed, and stress free
5. Maximize your learning style; visual learner use visual study aids, auditory learner use auditory study aids
6. Focus on your weakest knowledge base
7. Find a study partner to review with and help clarify questions
8. Practice, practice, practice
9. Get a good night's sleep; don't try to cram the night before the test
10. Eat a well balanced meal
11. Know the exact physical location of the testing site; drive the route to the site prior to test day
12. Bring a set of ear plugs; the testing center could be noisy
13. Wear comfortable, loose fitting, layered clothing to the testing center; prepare for it to be either cold or hot during the test
14. Bring at least 2 current forms of ID to the testing center
15. Arrive to the test early; be prepared to wait and be patient
16. Eliminate the obviously wrong answer choices, then guess the first remaining choice
17. Pace yourself; don't rush, but keep working and move on if you get stuck
18. Maintain a positive attitude even if the test is going poorly
19. Keep your first answer unless you are positive it is wrong
20. Check your work, don't make a careless mistake

Historical Development

NVGA

The National Vocational Guidance Association (NVGA) was established in 1913. It was the first professional organization bringing guidance counselors together and affirming their professional identity. It also began providing a publication for the sharing of ideas within the profession.

Clifford Beers

Clifford Beers graduated from Yale in 1897. Three years later, in 1900, he was hospitalized for the first of several times for depression and paranoia. Beers personally experienced and witnessed many abuses during his hospitalizations, which he described in his book, A Mind That Found Itself, published in 1908. The book found great acceptance and inspired reforms in the treatment of the mentally ill. Beers used the influence of his book to raise money for the founding of the Connecticut Committee on Mental Hygiene in 1908 and the National Committee on Mental Hygiene in 1909, both focused on reforming the inhumane treatment of the mentally ill.

Philippe Pinel

Born in 1745, Philippe Pinel was a French physician of internal medicine. Pinel's work as the chief physician at the French Bicêtre Hospital, beginning in 1793, brought about the first major reforms in the inhumane treatment of the mentally ill. Pinel ended bleeding, purging, and blistering treatments and began treatments focused on close patient contact, lengthy conversation, regular access to sunshine, and giving work or other meaningful activities to the patients. His close patient contact and lengthy conversation were not only therapeutic but also part of his efforts to study mental illness and understand the history and experience of his patients. In 1795, Pinel became the chief physician at the Hospice de la Salpêtrière, a village-like hospital for approximately 7,000 women, where Pinel instituted similar reforms and practices as he had at Bicêtre.

Wilhelm Wundt

Wilhelm Wundt (1832-1920), a German physician, psychologist, and physiologist, is known as the "father of experimental psychology." Wundt's early years of formal study and work covered the areas of medicine, physiology, and psychology, including teaching a class in "scientific psychology," in which he emphasized the use of empirical methods to study the human mind and behavior. His most famous contribution was the founding of the first laboratory for experimental psychology at the University of Leipzig, in 1879. While most of Wundt's conceptualizations of psychology have been discarded today, his introduction of empirical methods to the study of psychology is credited with separating psychology from philosophy as a distinct, independent field of study.

Frank Parsons

Frank Parsons (1854-1908) was a man of broad experience, training, and work in the fields of civil engineering, law, teaching, social reform, and vocational guidance counseling. His final career, guidance counseling, began in 1905 when he became the director of the Breadwinner's Institute, a program with the Civic Service House in Boston. Parsons is best known for founding the Bureau of Vocational Guidance in Boston in 1908, the year he died. The Bureau's mission was to help young people

- 14 -

finishing school find work. During these years, Parsons developed an approach to vocational guidance based on three fundamental concerns: 1) understanding of self; 2) understanding of work; and 3) determining the connection of the two through reasoning. His ideas were recorded in his influential book on vocational guidance counseling, Choosing a Vocation, published in 1909, the year after his death.

NDEA

On October 4, 1957, the Soviet Union successfully launched its first satellite, Sputnik I. This event generated significant concerns in the United States about competing with the Soviet Union in technology development and the fundamental education of the country's youth, especially in math and science. In 1958, the National Defense Education Act (NDEA) was passed. While the goals and funding of the NDEA were broad, its primary purpose was to improve education in math and science. Funding was directed to help schools: 1) identify academically gifted students, especially those with aptitudes in math and science; and 2) improve educational programs and facilities. It was the first goal that led to a significant increase in school guidance counselors throughout the nation.

Carl Rogers

Carl Rogers (1902-1987) was a significant influence in changing the way many thought about counseling. Prior to the presentation of his ideas about counseling, originally called nondirective therapy, conventional paradigms of counseling were directive, with the "expert" counselor guiding the client in the healing and change process. In contrast, Rogers' approach emphasized listening to and understanding the client. Rogers also placed new emphasis on such things as expressing empathy and

reflecting the client's words with attention to feelings and experience. Rogers' approach, later called client-centered therapy and now also called person-centered therapy, was brought to the national scene in his book, Client-Centered Therapy: Its Current Practice, Implications and Theory. In essence, Rogers' contribution to counseling was to bring a new focus on the importance of the therapeutic relationship.

Counseling organizations

The 1950s saw the creation of two new professional organizations for counselors and the renaming of a third. The two new associations were the American Personnel and Guidance Association (APGA) and the American School Counselor Association (ASCA). The APGA was established in 1952 from a number of existing organizations—including the National Vocational Guidance Association (NVGA)—that had been loosely connected via the Council of Guidance and Personnel Associations (CGPA). The ASCA was formed in 1953 and joined the APGA later that same year. Additionally, in 1951, the American Psychological Association (APA) changed the name of its Division 17 from Personnel and Guidance Psychologists to Counseling and Guidance. Just two years later, in 1953, the name was changed to Counseling Psychology.

B.F. Skinner

Burrhus Frederic Skinner, more commonly identified as B.F. Skinner, made many significant contributions to the fields of psychology and counseling. While behavior had been studied prior to Skinner, most notably by Ivan Pavlov and E.L. Thorndike, Skinner's theories and principles were major factors in the advancement of behavioral psychology and the establishment of behavioral therapy in the late 1950s. Foremost of

- 15 -

Skinner's contributions are the principles of operant conditioning, which have gained broad acceptance and application in therapy and elsewhere. Operant conditioning, in essence, is the shaping of behavior through the systematic changing of consequences. While Skinner wrote many books, two of his most influential are among his earliest: Science and Human Behavior (1953) and Schedules of Reinforcement (1957, cowritten with C.B. Ferster).

Counselor training standardization

The standardization of counselor training had its official beginning in 1981 with the establishment of the Council for Accreditation of Counseling and Related Educational Programs (CACREP). In 1979, the National Academy for Certified Mental Health Counselors (NACCMHC) was formed by the American Mental Health Counselors Association (AMHCA) and began offering a certification as a Certified Clinical Mental Health Counselor (CCMHC). In 1982, the National Board of Certified Counselors (NBCC) was formed, giving all counselors a recognized and respected means of certification: the National Certified Counselor (NCC) certification. In 1987, CACREP joined the Council on Postsecondary Accreditation (COPA), strengthening the value of its accreditations. Finally, in 1993, the NBCC and NACCMHC developed an agreement for NBCC to offer the CCMHC credential as a specialty certification available only to those who had already obtained the NCC credential.

E.G. Williamson

Working from Frank Parsons' ideas about vocational guidance, E.G. Williamson developed the first comprehensive theory of counseling, offering application to counseling in general, not just vocational guidance. His trait and factor theory of counseling was presented, in 1939, in his book, How to Counsel Students: A Manual of Techniques for Clinical Counselors. In essence, Williamson's approach is counselor-directed problem solving. The core of trait and factor counseling involves five basic steps: 1) analysis; 2) synthesis; 3) diagnosis; 4) counseling; and 5) follow-up. While initially inspired by and focused on vocational guidance, this broader problem-solving approach allowed the theory to be applied to non-vocational concerns and to gain its recognition as the first general counseling theory.

ACA

The American Counseling Association's (ACA) origins are found in four professional vocational guidance organizations that came together in 1952 to form the American Personnel and Guidance Association (APGA). By the 1970s, the number of non-vocational counselors had increased significantly, especially those working in community mental health centers. These counselors, however, had no national professional organization with which to identify. Recognizing this need, in 1976 the APGA formed a division called the American Mental Health Counseling Association (AMHCA). By the 1980s, the APGA's membership had changed significantly and most members were not working in the personnel or guidance fields. In response, in 1983 the APGA changed its name to the American Association for Counseling and Development (AACD). Finally, in 1992, to simplify its recognition as the professional organization for all counselors, the AACD changed its name to the American Counseling Association.

While primarily servicing counselors in the United States, the American Counseling Association (ACA) is the largest professional organization for counselors in the world. The ACA has 19 charter divisions. The most prominent of its divisions are the American Mental Health Counselors Association (AMHCA), the American College Counseling Association (ACCA), the American School Counselor Association (ASCA), the Association for Specialists in Group Work (ASGW), and the International Association of Marriage and Family Counselors (IAMFC). The ACA's flagship journal, published for all members, is the *Journal of Counseling & Development*. Ten other journals are published by ACA divisions.

Counselor Roles and Functions

MFTs

While they are most broadly considered members of the counseling profession, marriage and family therapists (MFTs) have several distinctions from other counselors. MFTs have their own professional organization—the American Association for Marriage and Family Therapy (AAMFT)—and their own standards, ethics code, and licensing. However, MFTs may and do obtain the National Certified Counselor (NCC) credential available through the National Board of Certified Counselors (NBCC). MFTs earn a master's degree (or, for some, a doctorate) in MFT, not counseling. The major distinction of MFTs is their primary theoretical orientation on family systems theory. While MFTs may do individual counseling, their primary mode of counseling is with couples and families—and when doing individual counseling, they will place considerable emphasis on assessment of and attention to the family system.

The two professional organizations representing marriage and family counselors are the American Association for Marriage and Family Therapy (AAMFT) and the International Association of Marriage and Family Counselors (IAMFC). The IAMFC is a division of the American Counseling Association (ACA). Each organization promotes separate standards for training in this professional specialization. The AAMFT promotes and controls its standards through the Commission on Accreditation for Marriage and Family Therapy Education (COAMFTE). In contrast, the IAMFC standards are administered by the Council for Accreditation of Counseling and Related Educational Programs (CACREP).

Social workers

Social workers are, in many ways, quite similar to professional counselors. While social workers often do clinical work similar to counseling, their core training and typical practice are oriented on social agencies, social systems, and government programs. Their mode of work is quite varied, including case management, administration, and clinical social work, the latter being essentially the same work as counseling. Social workers may hold a bachelor's degree, master's degree, or doctorate in social work; although, in most states, at least a master's degree is required to do clinical work comparable to professional counseling.

Psychologists

While some professional counselors obtain a doctor of counseling degree, most are master's-level professionals. In contrast, psychologists must earn doctoral-level degrees. Psychologists' training and practice cover many areas, including clinical, counseling, and education. In practice, the strength of their training gives them two key areas of professional dominance: 1) research; and 2) psychometric testing and diagnosis. While counselors do contribute to research in mental health, psychologists conduct the majority of mental health research. The average counselor's training in and experience with psychological testing is much more limited than that of psychologists. Consequently, counselors often refer testing to a psychologist, especially for more sophisticated tests.

Psychiatrists

Psychiatrists' greatest distinction from all other mental health professionals is that they are medical doctors. After receiving a degree in medicine, they gain additional training in mental health through a residency in psychiatry. Their training in medicine and psychiatry is much more medical-model and biologically oriented than the training of other mental health professionals. In practice, psychiatrists frequently, if not primarily, rely on prescribing medicine to address mental health concerns. While some psychiatrists will counsel their patients in long conversational sessions similar to professional counselors, most do not. It is not uncommon for psychiatrists to spend only 15 or 20 minutes with patients during their visits.

Paraprofessional and ministerial counselors

Many forms of paraprofessional and ministerial helping relationships share similarities with professional counseling, including the word *counselor*. These paraprofessional vocations include caseworkers, mental health technicians, probation officers, and childcare workers. In general, these types of helpers usually have some formal training in human services. Ministerial relationships sharing similarities with counseling include pastors, volunteer youth workers, and lay counselors. Pastors have varied education levels and some may have some formal training in counseling, but all generally have legally protected rights to counsel members or attendees of their churches. Churches also sometimes have volunteer lay counselors or youth workers providing informal counseling to other church members. While these types of paraprofessional and ministerial relationships perform functions somewhat similar to those of counselors, professional counselors are clearly distinguished by their advanced formal training, professional standards, ethics codes, certification, and licensure.

Multidisciplinary teams

Multidisciplinary mental health treatment teams usually comprise three to six people with diverse training and expertise. The cumulative expertise of a treatment team often makes it easier to treat a client in a more holistic and comprehensive way. Multidisciplinary teams typically comprise some of the following types of helpers: counselors, psychologists, psychiatrists, social workers, nurses, physical therapists, occupational therapists, physiotherapists, dieticians, nutritionists, caseworkers, and mental health technicians. Special situations may see teachers, pastors, lawyers, or others be invited to participate on a treatment team for a specific client, depending on the specific situation. While multidisciplinary teams may be found just about anywhere they are deemed appropriate, common settings include hospitals, community mental health centers (CMHCs), outpatient clinics, schools, and substance abuse clinics.

MHC

A mental health counselor (MHC) is a master's- or doctoral-level counselor with broad training and many potential work settings. In many ways, MHCs represent the most generalized profession in mental health care. Training typically includes an introduction to most counseling theories, including family systems theories. MHCs are also trained in career counseling, community counseling, human development, psychometrics, psychopharmacology, and substance abuse and addictions counseling. The training of MHCs will typically place more emphasis than that of other types of counselors on assessment and diagnosis from the psychiatric-based Diagnostic and Statistical Manual (DSM). However, mental health counseling is much more developmentally and wellness oriented than psychiatry. Potential work settings for MHCs include most environments where counselors may work. While all MHCs start with broad, general training, many develop specializations as their careers progress.

Surveys

A survey attempts to answer a research question by the simple solicitation or collection of information about a given sample population. Information may be collected by in-person interviews, telephone interviews, or written questionnaires (mailed or in-person), or by pulling information from existing records. The research samples may be evaluated either at one point in time, *cross-sectional*, or at multiple points in time, *longitudinal.* Written surveys can be especially efficient for research with large sample populations, especially when mailed. A limitation of mailed surveys is the lack of control over who returns the surveys and potential skewing of the sample population.

CACREP

Just as the types of counseling are varied, counselor education programs are also varied. The organization that provides standards and guidelines for the accreditation of most counseling programs is the Council for Accreditation of Counseling and Related Educational Programs (CACREP). CACREP accredits master's and doctoral degree programs in eight distinct professional counseling areas: mental health counseling; marital, couple, and family counseling/therapy; community counseling; career counseling; gerontological counseling; school counseling; college counseling; and counselor education and supervision.

Career counselors

Career counselors are professionals who help others with career- or job-related concerns. They work in a variety of settings, such as colleges, private practice, government employment offices, and vocational rehabilitation centers. They may also work as consultants for businesses or high schools, assisting employees or students in career planning. The core work of career counseling involves assessing clients and their situations, helping clients think about vocational concerns, and assisting them in vocational decisions. A key element of this work involves testing and assessment of clients' vocational education, training, skills, interests, experiences, and attitudes. Career counselors, like other counselors, also need understanding of and skills related to mental health issues. Sometimes, mental health issues (e.g., depression) are significant factors in a client's vocational concerns, and must be understood and addressed competently by the career counselor. Particular emphasis may be given to understanding and treating stress and anxiety related to workplace demands.

School counselors

School counselors are those counselors working in an elementary or high school setting. Although less frequently now, school counselors are sometimes also called guidance counselors. Elementary school counselors observe children in learning and play activities to assess a child's strengths, problems, or special needs. Elementary counselors may also work with school administrators in the development of school curricula to meet the developmental needs of the students. They may also help children with personal, social, or behavioral problems. High school counselors are primarily focused on helping students understand and plan their vocational direction. They provide information and advise students on college, trade, or technical school selection. They provide assessment testing to assist in career planning. High school counselors also advise students on practical matters such as application processes, entrance exams, and financial aid. Like elementary school counselors, high school counselors may also help students with personal, social, or behavioral problems.

College counselors

College counselors are any counselors working in a setting of higher education, from the largest universities to the smallest community colleges and technical schools. While recognized by the Council for Accreditation of Counseling and Related Educational Programs (CACREP) as a distinct educational program for accreditation, in practice, college counseling is a somewhat broad field. The primary concerns of almost all college counselors are student development and vocational guidance. From a student-development perspective, counselors help students deal with the challenges of this phase of life, such as identity, independence, and newly incurred adult responsibilities. College counselors also focus on helping students connect their academic choices to an end career goal. Some college counselors will also help students with personal or mental health concerns; others will simply refer students to other counselors for these needs. A college counselor working in a student affairs office may have significant administrative duties, in addition to counseling.

Substance abuse counselors

Substance abuse and addictions counselors work with clients struggling with the destructive behaviors of abuse and addiction to alcohol and drugs. In some cases, these skills in addictions

treatment are more broadly applied to include non-substance addictions such as gambling, work, eating, and pornography. Substance abuse and addictions counselors work in a variety of settings, some of the most common being addictions clinics, community mental health centers, and homeless shelters. While counseling is done on both individual and group levels, group counseling is usually considered more critical and effective for the treatment of addictions. Much of addictions counseling is done only in a group setting.

CMHC

Community mental health centers (CMHCs) were originally established nationwide in 1963 by the Community Mental Health Centers Act. These centers offer outpatient services for a wide variety of needs, as well as 24-hour emergency care services. CMHC services are available to the general public; however, the core service populations are the chronically mentally ill, those suffering from substance abuse and addiction, and the low-income population. In support of the low-income population, most CMHCs are certified Medicare and Medicaid centers.

The staff of a CMHC usually comprises at least one psychologist and one psychiatrist, counselors, social workers, nurses, caseworkers, mental health technicians, and administrative support personnel. The clinical director of a CMHC is usually a psychologist. Many services in a CMHC are supported by the multidisciplinary team approach, where the counselor is collaborating with other professionals in the service of their clients.

Laboratory and field research

Laboratory research is conducted in a controlled laboratory environment. Research conducted in a laboratory is

- 21 -

done for the benefits of eliminating and controlling variables. Critics of laboratory research often claim that laboratory environments are too artificial and human behavior cannot be expected to occur as it normally would in such environments. Critics of laboratory research in counseling usually favor field research because the behavior observed is expected to authentic. Field research includes all research conducted in "real life," not in a laboratory. However, in practice, most field research is done in a counseling setting. Critics of field research may also claim that, as with laboratory research, counseling settings are also artificial and may not support observation of authentic behavior in the research subjects.

Quantitative and qualitative research

Quantitative research is primarily objective and reproducible, and can be reduced to numerical and statistical data. In contrast, qualitative research is more subjective, sacrificing reproducibility and quantification in favor of flexibility and an unconstrained pursuit of understanding. The constraints of quantitative research promote basic scientific fundamentals such as the study of cause and effect, standardized measures, and statistical analysis. Due to its nature, qualitative research is often focused on an individual or small group. In contrast, quantitative research can potentially be applied to sample groups of almost any size, limited only by practical constraints. Two basic forms of quantitative research are experiments and surveys. Typical forms of qualitative research include case studies, interviews, and life histories.

NBCC

The National Board for Certified Counselors (NBCC) is the leading organization for the certification of counselors in the United States. The NBCC's general counselor certification and the one sought by most counselors is the National Certified Counselor (NCC) certificate. The major requirement for obtaining the NCC is passing the National Counselor Examination (NCE). The NCC certification is the major national credential for identifying counselors who meet the basic standards of the counseling profession. The NBCC also offers three specialty certifications:

- The National Certified School Counselor (NCSC) certificate
- The Certified Clinical Mental Health Counselor (CCMHC) certificate
- The Master Addictions Counselor (MAC) certificate.

Earning the NCC is a prerequisite for each specialty certification.

Counselors as consultants

Whereas counseling is usually oriented on promoting growth and addressing personal concerns of individuals, couples, and families, consulting is typically focused on training and problem solving. Unlike counseling, consulting is usually performed at a school, business, or agency, not in the counselor's office. In the consulting relationship, goals, time frames, and compensation are rigidly defined and established in a contract. In a training consultation, the counselor is being contracted to teach a specific set of expert knowledge and skills to an individual or group. In a problem-solving consultation, the counselor is being contracted either: 1) to assess and provide recommended solutions to a problem; or 2) to guide individuals, groups, or organizations in solving their own problems. Some consultation work may be a combination of the two.

Problem-solving consultation models

Expert model – In the expert model, the counselor works independently in assessing and solving a problem for the client.

Mediation model – In the mediation model, the counselor works with a group or organization to solve a problem. The counselor provides guidance in helping the various individuals or groups to work together in solving the problem. Alternatively, the counselor may assess the situation and advise a solution to the problem that is agreeable to all concerned parties.

Process consultation – In the process consultation model, the counselor acts as a guide helping clients work through the problem-solving process and allowing clients to develop their own solutions.

ASGW group types

The Association for Specialists in Group Work identifies four types of groups in their training standards as follows:

Task and work group facilitation – Group work in which counselors facilitate a group process in accomplishing an identified task.

Psychoeducation group leadership – Group work in which counselors teach psychologically based content and skills to promote personal growth, help group members deal with personal issues, or prevent future problems.

Group counseling – Group work in which counselors help group members in dealing with non-severe, non-chronic difficulties of life such as grief, divorce, or job loss. Personal growth and change are also typical goals.

Group psychotherapy – Group work in which counselors help group members in dealing with severe and/or chronic psychological problems or dysfunction. Major changes in thinking, behavior, or personality are the primary goals. Personal growth is a common secondary goal.

Group development

The five stages of group development developed by Bruce Tuckman are as follows:

1. *Forming*: The group comes together and begins getting to know one another. Group rules and expectations are established. Relationships remain superficial.
2. *Storming*: Group discussion and relationships begin to move to a deeper level. Minor conflict will begin to occur. Group members are now trying to establish their place or role in the group.
3. *Norming*: Informal and unspoken rules and norms for how the group operates are established. Most relationship conflicts are now settled with mutual understanding.
4. *Performing*: Group trust and loyalty are high. Group work is comfortable, efficient, and effective. Most relationships in the group are well established and require little mental or emotional energy to manage.
5. *Adjourning*: This is the process of ending the group. Group members say good-bye to each other. Good closure is important.

Open and closed groups

Open groups – Open groups allow new group members to join the group at any time. If the group has a maximum size, it may be temporarily "closed" until existing group members leave, creating room for new members to join. Open groups may last for years and are potentially "unending."

Closed groups – Closed groups do not allow new members to join after: 1) the group has begun; 2) a specified point early in its forming; or (3) a predetermined maximum number of group members is achieved. In the latter case, once a group has reached the predetermined size, the group will not admit new group members, even if group members leave, reducing the size of the group below the maximum number.

Therapy and support groups

Therapy groups are led by one or more counselors or other mental health professionals. Support groups are led by non-professionals. The leaders of support groups typically are dealing personally with the same issues as other group members: the issues that the group was formed to address. Therapy groups usually focus more on self-exploration and fostering therapeutic change. In contrast, support groups are usually focused on providing support, encouragement, and understanding from others with similar experiences. Sometimes the term *support group* is meant to refer only to groups sponsored by an organization (usually a mental health service provider). In such contexts, the term *self-help group* may be used to distinguish groups that are led by non-professionals but are not sponsored by an organization.

Structured and unstructured support groups

Structured groups have established patterns and expectations for what will be done in the group. Structured groups are usually guided by specific agendas for each session. Group exercises or organized activities may be used. Reading assignments or other homework are common elements in structured groups. In contrast, unstructured groups have no formally established patterns or expectations. Unstructured groups may have no agenda for a session, or a minimal, loosely defined agenda. Unstructured groups are process oriented. Discussion is stimulated and guided by the concerns and issues that

group members bring to the session for discussion. Unstructured groups tend to foster deeper discussion of issues and increased self-disclosure.

Family life cycle

The eight stages of the family life cycle according to Evelyn Duvall span from marriage to the death of both spouses. The eight stages are:
1. *Married couples* (without children): Establishing the marriage relationship; realignment of relationships with extended family and friends.
2. *Childbearing families* (oldest child, birth–30 months): Making adjustments for the new child; learning to parent; parents adjust to their parents' new role as grandparents.
3. *Preschool-aged children* (oldest child, 2½–6 years): Adapting to the shifting demands of parenting and learning the child's changing needs.
4. *School-aged children* (oldest child, 6–13 years): Focus shifts to the child's education; parents learn to deal with increased activity and demands of the child; child begins developing significant relationships outside the family.
5. *Teenagers* (oldest child, 13–20 years): Parents and teenager adapt to the increasing independence of the teenager; parents learn to adjust to mid-life challenges of family and career.
6. *Families as launching centers* (first child gone to last child leaving home): Child is released into adult life; parents and child learn to relate in new adult-to-adult relationship; parents provide support as children learn to establish themselves as independent adults; possible adjustments to children's spouses

and new grandchildren entering the family.

7. *Middle-aged parents* ("empty nest" to retirement): A renewed focus and additional energy are given to the marriage relationship; parents continue to accept children's spouses and new grandchildren into the family; the middle-aged parents are now dealing with the aging and possible support of their own parents.

8. *Aging family members* (retirement to death of both spouses): entering retirement; coping with the death of parents and spouse.

Marriage, couple, and family counseling

The four phases in the process of marriage, couple, and family counseling are:

1. *Pre-counseling*: A member of the marriage or family contacts the counselor to request counseling. The potential client states a summary of why counseling is being sought. The counselor listens carefully for initial clues to family or couple relationship dynamics.

2. *Initial session(s)*: The counselor begins initial assessment of the family or couple's context and stated concerns. The counselor focuses on assessing relationship dynamics. The counselor makes an effort to establish rapport and trust with each family member.

3. *Middle phase*: Ideally, trust and rapport are well established. Initial assessment is completed and the counselor has clear conceptualizations of the family system and possible therapeutic interventions to create lasting change. The counselor begins challenging the family to new ways of behaving and relating.

4. *Termination*: The counselor reviews and summarizes counseling. Guidance is given for continued success after counseling. A follow-up session may be scheduled.

Family systems theory

Family systems theory is a broad, overarching theory, which is foundational to much of modern family counseling. Systems theory suggests that a system has properties that the individual parts of the system do not. Systems theory is focused on dynamic interactions of the system, not on the isolated actions of individual parts. Thus, family systems theory encourages counselors to focus on the dynamics of family relationships, not individual behavior. In family systems theory, the simple linear concept of cause and effect is replaced by *circular causality*, the idea that actions and reactions play back and forth on each other, potentially unending. This focus is applied not just to relationships between two people, but to all members of the family, and invites consideration of complex interactions. Further, families are seen as *open systems*, meaning that outside influences may affect the system, and so family counselors may consider sociocultural influences on the family system.

Advocacy

Counselors may advocate for both the counseling profession and client concerns by engaging the political and legislative processes to promote or prevent the passage of laws, as appropriate. Counselors can maintain awareness of ongoing legislative efforts by maintaining association with a professional organization and following the organization's tracking of key legislative concerns. The American Counseling Association's (ACA) Office of Public Policy and Information is a key example of such a conduit.

The most effective ways counselors can take personal action in the promotion or opposition of bills is by writing letters and meeting with legislators. Another effective way for counselors to engage in advocacy is to become involved with the ongoing efforts of their professional organizations.

Rehabilitation counselor

A rehabilitation counselor works with clients who have disabilities. Rehabilitation counselors help clients learn to live effectively with the challenges of their disabilities, as well as with mental and emotional issues that may be of concern. Rehabilitation counselors work in a wide variety of settings, including government rehabilitation offices, private rehabilitation programs, mental health centers, hospitals, schools, independent learning centers, and insurance companies. Activities and functions of the specialty are broad. In addition to basic counseling, other functions include coordinating services, case management, vocational guidance, job placement and training, visiting the client's home for assessment of living situation and needs, and visiting the client's workplace to assess needs for disability assistance.

College counseling models

The four major models of college counseling services are:
- *Vocational guidance*: The focus of the vocational guidance model is on helping students identify career goals and connect them to their academic choices. Mental health and developmental concerns of the student are referred by the college counselor to another service provider.

- *Counseling as psychotherapy*: In contrast, and nearly opposite of the vocational guidance model, this model of counseling focuses on student developmental and mental health concerns. Student issues related to vocational guidance and academics are referred by the counselor to student academic advisers.
- *Consultation*: This model is focused on early identification and prevention of both personal and academic/vocational issues. The counselor works to coordinate interventions with relevant entities in the student's educational experience, such as faculty, staff, and campus organizations.
- *Traditional counseling*: This model is, in many ways, a combination of the other three. The counselor may address developmental, mental health, academic, and vocational concerns of the student.

Counselor credentials

Certification in counseling, or a counseling specialty, is achieved by completing a set of given requirements from a certifying organization. Certifications simply communicate that a counselor has met the standards necessary for a given certification, and are only as good as the reputation of the certification. Standards for certification usually include passing an exam. Generally, certifications have no legal bearing. In contrast, licensure permits legal practice at a legally defined level. In the counseling profession, nearly all licensure is controlled and administered at the state level. Qualifying for licensure typically requires passing an exam. Registration is a less significant and less common form of legal recognition by a state. To be registered, a counselor simply submits information demonstrating the required level of training and experience.

Supervision

Supervision is simply the process by which a counselor is supervised by another, more experienced counselor. Most counseling programs require some level of supervised counseling experience as a requirement for completing a degree. All programs accredited by the Council on Accreditation of Counseling and Related Education Programs (CACREP) have a supervision requirement. In a counseling education program, supervision is typically done by faculty in the program. State requirements for licensure typically require a specified number of hours of supervision to qualify for licensure. These requirements usually dictate that the supervisor currently holds the license being sought or another qualifying license. For instance, a counselor seeking a license as a mental health counselor may be allowed to receive supervision from other licensed mental health professionals, such as psychologists or social workers.

Consultation

The five stages of consultation as described by Dick Dustin and Stewart Ehly are:

1. *Phasing in*: Initial assessment of the consultation project is made and the counselor communicates professional qualifications for the project. The counselor and client discuss the needs and goals of the consultation.
2. *Problem identification*: The nature and details of the consultation project are refined and clearly determined. If appropriate, a contract for consultation is drafted.

3. *Implementation*: Problem analysis is conducted. Problem analysis is reviewed and discussed. A plan to solve the problem is made and executed.
4. *Follow-up and evaluation*: The results of the consultation process are evaluated. If the client is dissatisfied, the counselor and client may agree to additional consultation work.
5. *Termination*: The consulting relationship is ended. The process is reviewed and relevant feedback is offered. Terms for future follow-up may be defined.

Counseling research

Basic research – Basic research is oriented on theory and attempts to answers questions suggested by an existing theory. *Applied research* – In contrast to basic research, applied research is oriented on practical concerns of counseling and attempts to provide a better understanding of or solutions to those practical concerns. *Process research* – Process research is focused on how counseling is done, or on the counseling process. It evaluates what is done in a counseling session by both counselor and client. *Outcome research* – In contrast to process research, outcome research is focused on the results of counseling. Measurements and subjective survey information are collected at both the beginning and end of the counseling process. Research analysis is concerned with the change that occurs from before to after counseling.

Core curricular areas

The Council for Accreditation of Counseling and Related Educational Programs (CACREP) has established eight core curricular areas that are required for accredited counseling programs. They are:

1. *Professional orientation and ethical practice*: Provides instruction in professional aspects such as the history of counseling, roles and responsibilities, professional organizations and credentialing, and ethical and legal concerns.
2. *Social and cultural diversity*: Provides instruction to promote understanding of cultural diversity in the context of counseling relationships.
3. *Human growth and development*: Provides instruction in the understanding of human development across the life span.
4. *Career development*: Provides instruction in the theories and models of career development, processes, and techniques for helping clients make career decisions.
5. *Helping relationships*: Provides instruction in skills and theories for managing an effective counseling relationship.
6. *Group work*: Provides instruction and experiential learning in group counseling. Emphasis is given to the inclusion of an experiential component.
7. *Assessment*: Provides instruction in assessment and evaluation of the client, with significant orientation on psychometric principles.
8. *Research and program evaluation*: Provides instruction in research methods, statistical analysis, needs assessment, and program evaluation.

Case study

A case study is a research method used to do focused, intensive studies of just one person, group, organization, or program. A case study may involve careful design and controls in research on a major program, or a case study may simply be based on a counselor's sessions with a client and the counselor's session notes. However, in case studies like the latter, the observations and findings of the case study may be viewed as less reliable. Case studies are inherently *longitudinal*, meaning that the research on the given sample occurs over a period of time. The benefits of case studies to counseling are: 1) they can potentially be conducted with minimal cost and resources; and 2) they easily facilitate in-depth examination of individual clients or programs.

Experimental research

Experimental research is a method of research used to determine cause and effect. This type of research is designed around a *hypothesis*, an unproven notion of cause and effect, and is focused on two factors: the *independent variable* and the *dependent variable*. The independent variable is purposefully manipulated by the researcher and the dependent variable is observed and recorded to determine the effect of the varying independent variable. To allow for reliable cause-and-effect analysis, the researcher attempts to design the study so that all other factors are eliminated or controlled. Typical independent variables in counseling would be different types of treatments, or a specific variable of treatment. Respectively, typical dependent variables would be the outcomes of treatment or specific characteristics of treatment outcomes. Two advantages of experimental research are that it: 1) is quantifiable; and 2) can readily be applied to large sample sizes.

Statistical concepts

Median – In a set of numerical data sorted in rank order, the median is the exact middle value or midpoint. In an even numbered set of data, there will be two median values.

Mean – The mean is the mathematical average of a set of numerical data. The mean is calculated by summing the values in the data set and dividing by the number of values in the data set.

Mode – The mode is the value that occurs the most often in a data set.

Standard deviation – Standard deviation is the measure of variability around the mean in a data set. A smaller standard deviation means values do not vary greatly from the mean value. In contrast, a larger standard deviation indicates a larger dispersal of values around the mean.

The Counseling Relationship

Nonverbal communication

Much of the communication that takes place in a counseling relationship is not done with words. Some research has even suggested that the majority of human communication is nonverbal. Nonverbal communication consists of all the information and signals communicated apart from words, but does also include characteristics of speech. Common examples of nonverbal communication include eye contact, hand gestures, facial expressions, crossed arms and legs, foot tapping, shoulder shrugging, head nodding, body lean, smiling, tone of voice, vocal inflection, and volume of speech. Nonverbal and verbal communication often conflict. When this happens, people usually (and often subconsciously) trust the nonverbal and do not believe the words spoken. An intentional example of this conflict is sarcasm. Counselors who pay attention to nonverbals may often see their clients communicating something different from what their words communicate. An example is the client who says, "I'm fine," while avoiding eye contact and fidgeting because he is really quite depressed but is not comfortable acknowledging it yet.

Helpful counselor behavior

A counselor's behavior, both verbal and nonverbal, in counseling is key to developing a good counseling relationship. Helpful counselor behaviors will communicate friendliness, understanding, acceptance, empathy, attentiveness, and caring. Key verbal behaviors that are helpful are:

- paraphrasing and clarifying client statements to demonstrate careful listening and understanding
- communicating acceptance in response to statements imbued with shame or guilt
- offering observations or comments that indicate a depth of understanding
- using verbal reinforcers like "Yes" and "Mm-hmm" that communicate attentiveness.

Key nonverbal counselor behaviors that are helpful are:

- good eye contact, which communicates attentiveness and caring
- smiling, which communicates acceptance and friendliness
- forward body lean, which communicates interest and concern
- head nodding, a nonverbal reinforcer, communicating attentiveness.

Unhelpful counselor behavior

A counselor's behavior, both verbal and nonverbal, can potentially be harmful to a developing counseling relationship. Such unhelpful counselor behaviors may communicate disinterest, misunderstanding, or rejection. Key verbal behaviors that are unhelpful are:

- interrupting, which may communicate poor listening and lack of respect
- blaming, which may communicate misunderstanding or judgment
- extensive questioning (especially "why" questions), which may make a client guarded
- minimizing, which invalidates a client's statement or concern.

Key nonverbal counselor behaviors that are unhelpful are:

- poor eye contact, which may communicate disinterest or lack of caring
- frowning or rigid facial expressions
- acting rushed, suggesting the counselor does not have time for the client
- yawning, which may communicate disinterest.

Goals

It is important that goals are identified and agreed to early in the counseling relationship. Goals help to ensure that both the counselor and client are working to achieve the same objective, and they provide a common focus and direction. Goals are particularly useful in aiding continuity from one session to the next. Goals may change in the counseling process, as needed, when agreed to by both counselor and client. Goals may be formally recorded in a treatment plan or other documents detailing the key elements of the counseling relationship. Ideally, goals are specific, observable, measurable, and achievement oriented.

Treatment plan

A treatment plan is a cornerstone document in counseling, clarifying and recording key elements of assessment and intent in the counseling relationship. A treatment plan records the following major elements:

- Assessment of client issues, concerns, or symptomatic features: This assessment may include issues that have been identified but will not be specifically addressed in counseling. Some concerns may be identified by some clinicians as dysfunction, disorders, or

psychopathology. This section may also include a basic assessment of previous mental health and physical diagnoses, sociocultural context, and key elements of client history.
- Goals or objectives to be achieved: In addition to the desired outcome of counseling, this section may include short-term, intermediate goals in the counseling process.
- Techniques and interventions: This section describes what the counselor intends to do to address the issues and goals identified; in other words, it describes the plan for treatment.

Transference and countertransference

The concepts of transference and countertransference were originally developed in psychoanalytic theory. However, the basic concepts apply to all counseling and provide a guide for careful consideration in the counseling relationship. Transference refers to client feelings and attitudes directed towards the counselor based on relationships from the client's past. Recognizing transference is important for the counselor for both assessment and good communication. First, transference may indicate important issues that need to be addressed. Second, transference may cause the client to "filter" or distort what a counselor does and says. Countertransference refers to the emotions and behaviors of the counselor in response to the client. While countertransference is not inherently harmful, it can be. Two potential concerns are when the counselor's feelings or behaviors deteriorate client trust or therapeutic objectivity.

Premature termination

Premature termination means the client has decided to end counseling prior to resolving her original concerns or before the agreed-to goals of counseling have been achieved. Possible reasons for premature termination are endless, but common reasons include:

- The client does not feel that counseling is helping.
- The counseling process produces anxiety the client wants to avoid.
- The client wants to see if the counselor cares about him.
- The client does not feel understood by the counselor.

A counselor can do many things to reduce the likelihood of premature termination; some of the most important include:

- courtesy reminders of counseling appointments, such as letters, cards, phone calls, and emails
- scheduling regular appointments and avoiding long gaps between appointments
- careful attention to making sure the client feels understood in counseling, especially during early sessions.

Follow-up

Follow-up refers to counselor-initiated contact with the client after termination of counseling. While this is an often-neglected element of the counseling relationship, it can be valuable therapeutically for the client and provides helpful information for the counselor. Follow-up can help to clarify and emphasize the gains made in counseling for the client. It also reinforces the counselor's concern and caring for the client. The counselor benefits from follow-up through client feedback, which may clarify successes and limitations of the counseling process. Typical forms of follow-up include:

- The client returns for a follow-up session in the counselor's office.
- The counselor makes a telephone call to the client.
- The counselor sends a personal letter to the client.
- The counselor sends a follow-up questionnaire or survey. This latter method can be beneficial for long-term, comparative tracking of all of a counselor's clients.

Referral

A referral is when a counselor decides to refer a client to another service provider and end the existing counseling relationship. Essentially, referrals are made when the counselor decides that continuing the counseling relationship is not in the best interests of the client. Counselors need to recognize that they cannot help every client who comes to them and be ready to make a referral when appropriate. Common reasons for referrals are:

- The counselor feels she cannot competently or adequately help the client.
- The counselor and client have a personal conflict or incompatible personalities.
- Counseling seems to be ineffective for reasons the counselor cannot determine and resolve.

Boundaries

Boundaries are those things that help define our relationships with others. They define how the relationship will work, determine what is acceptable and what is not, and indicate the roles we play in a relationship. In counseling, attention to boundaries is important to avoid potentially awkward or harmful situations. Two primary concerns are *boundary crossings* and *boundary violations*. Boundary crossings are deliberate adjustments to boundaries or changes in roles for the benefit of the client and the counseling process. For example, a counselor maintains a boundary of no hugging with clients, but makes a clinical decision to make an exception for a client when he decides there is an important emotional benefit and potential concerns are unlikely to occur. In contrast, a boundary violation is a breach of an understood relational boundary that is harmful to a client.

Structure

Structure is essentially giving a client an orientation to and understanding of how counseling will work. Structure is important to the success of counseling and promoting client trust, especially in the initial sessions. Structure gives the client the comfort of knowing what to expect. Ideally, counselors will give significant attention in the first session to explaining an outline of both the first session and the counseling process as a whole. A professional disclosure statement provided before or at the beginning of counseling is also useful in providing key information. Counselors should be prepared to receive and warmly invite questions from clients regarding how counseling will work and what they can expect. During this process, counselors may find that clients had very unrealistic and unreasonable expectations. A counselor's attention to orientation in early sessions will help to eliminate such problems.

Professional disclosure statement

A professional disclosure statement is used by a counselor to provide the client with initial information about the counselor and the counseling process. Key types of information provided include the qualifications and training of the counselor, fees and payment information, length of sessions, requirements for appointment cancellation, an explanation of confidentiality, and a description of counseling services and clinical approach. Because demonstrable proof that the client has received this information may be legally necessary in some situations, this form is typically signed by both the client and counselor. If the counselor is licensed or certified, license or certification numbers may be included in the section on qualifications. A well-written and informative professional disclosure statement will make the counselor's job of orientation in the first session much easier..

Client resistance

A resistant client is one who avoids or resists the counseling process or personal change. Such clients can be very difficult and frustrating for a counselor, but understanding the reasons for resistance may provide insights that assist the counselor in effectively overcoming initial resistance and helping the client. The reasons for client resistance are essentially unlimited, but typical examples include:

- The client has been ordered to counseling by the court, but does not believe she needs counseling.
- The client is a minor living with his parents and is being made to attend counseling by his parents, even though he insists that nothing is "wrong" and that he does not want to attend counseling.
- The client fears making personal change because of anticipated emotional pain.
- In marital counseling, a husband who attends counseling reluctantly because of emotional coercion by his wife.

Trust

Trust is a cornerstone in successful counseling. A client genuinely listening to and responding to a counselor depends on trust. Some key things that counselors can do to foster trust in the relationship are:

- providing good structure or orientation to the counseling process and establishing clear expectations; when a client experiences counseling differently from existing expectations, trust can be harmed.
- listening attentively to the client and demonstrating understanding through reflection, observations, and empathy.
- offering clear, strong messages of acceptance and compassion when the client dares to reveal shame- or guilt-laden personal information.

Self-disclosure

Self-disclosure is the disclosing of personal information to another person, with emphasis given to more sensitive and potentially compromising information. In counseling, *client* self-disclosure is expected for the process to work. In contrast, *counselor* self-disclosure is not expected, but may be therapeutically helpful in certain situations. Counselors may choose to offer limited self-disclosure in counseling for a variety of reasons, including:

- enhancing the client's sense that the counselor understands her situation and feelings.
- creating a sense of normalcy when the counselor perceives that the client believes his experience, thoughts, or feelings are highly abnormal or unusual.
- fostering and deepening client trust.

- promoting continuing or deepening client disclosure.

Personal characteristics and skills

There are many personal characteristics and skills of a counselor that can be identified as helpful to good counseling. While the degree of control may vary, most of these characteristics and skills can be cultivated and fostered to some extent. Key characteristics and skills that counselors may consider developing or correcting are:

- honesty
- good listening skills
- self-awareness
- empathy – the ability to understand another person despite differences in background and experience
- good communication skills
- comfort with intimacy – the ability to maintain a relationship with deep emotional and intimate content
- genuine interest in and concern for other people
- compassion – the ability to understand another person's suffering and desiring to help.

Physical setting

The physical setting of counseling, while often overlooked, can have a significant effect on the success of counseling. Characteristics of the physical setting that counseling occurs in have been identified as affecting client comfort, tendency for self-disclosure, trust, mood, and energy levels. Characteristics of the physical setting that should be considered include:

- *seating and tables*: comfortable and arrangement conducive to intimate conversation
- *room temperature and humidity*: most people are comfortable in

temperatures of 70–77º F and 30–60% relative humidity
- *noise*: both reducing distracting noises and deliberate use of white noise, from items like water fountains, to promote privacy
- *lighting*: research indicates that softer, lower lighting increases relaxation and self-disclosure in clients
- *color*: brighter colors promote a more positive mood
- *smell*: offensive or unpleasant smells can create distraction and reduce comfort
- *accessories*: items such as wall art and plants may affect the comfort and mood of the client.

Empathy

Empathy is the ability of a person to understand and connect on a meaningful level with another person's experience without the benefit of similar experience, feelings, or background. The ability to be truly empathetic involves two key skills: perception and communication. Perception has three primary elements: 1) careful, attentive listening; 2) a counselor's understanding of the feelings connected with the client's experience; and 3) the counselor's ability to understand and appreciate the client's cultural context. Accurate perception alone is not enough, because if the counselor cannot communicate his perception, the client will not experience empathy. The counselor must be able to express what he is hearing so that the client knows and believes that the counselor really understands.

Informed consent

Informed consent simply refers to the right of a client to be informed about counseling and its various elements before consenting to the process. It refers to both the beginning of counseling and during the ongoing process. This information is provided to the client by both written documents, such as a professional disclosure statement, and verbal explanations in counseling. For legal purposes, documents of informed consent are usually signed by both client and counselor. From a legal perspective, informed consent consists of three elements: *capacity*, *comprehension of information*, and *voluntariness*. These elements may be defined as follows:
- Capacity means the client is of a sound mind and able to make decisions for himself.
- Comprehension means the client accurately understands the information given.
- Voluntariness means the client is giving consent voluntarily, and not being forced or coerced.

Confidentiality

Confidentiality is the ethical responsibility of the counselor to protect the personal information that a client discloses in counseling. Confidentiality is the bedrock of counseling. Clients disclose deeply personal and vulnerable information in counseling because they expect it to stay there. Essentially all mental health professions address the importance of confidentiality in their ethics codes. In general, confidentiality is maintained except when: 1) the client requests that the counselor provide confidential information to another person or organization; or 2) the counselor is legally required or authorized to disclose confidential information.

Confidentiality limitations

While confidentiality is critical in counseling, it does have limitations. Counselors have an important ethical (and, in some cases, legal) obligation to explain the limitations of confidentiality at the beginning of counseling. Exceptions may always be made, of course, if the client requests it. Other legal and ethical exceptions to confidentiality include:

- limited access to confidential information by administrative staff supporting the counselor
- minimal disclosure necessary to obtain third-party reimbursement for services
- counselor supervision
- court orders legally mandating disclosure
- the counselor's duty to warn or protect; disclosure, as necessary, to prevent harm to the client or others.

Warn and protect

One of the key limitations to confidentiality in counseling is the counselor's duty to warn and protect. Essentially, the counselor may have legal and ethical obligations to disclose information in order to protect the client or others from harm. This duty, in its various aspects, has been legally established by the verdicts of various court cases and is recognized in nearly all states. The kinds of situations in which this duty applies include the following:

- A counselor reasonably believes a client may attempt suicide and discloses information, as necessary, to enable others to prevent the client from killing himself.
- A client indicates he is going to kill or violently harm someone and the counselor discloses information, as necessary, to authorities, family, or friends to protect the potential victim.
- A counselor reasonably believes that a child (or children) is being abused or neglected and reports information to child protective services and others to protect the child (or children).

Privileged communication

Privileged communication is a legal concept related to confidentiality. Privileged communication protects against forced disclosure of a client's confidential information during legal proceedings. Privileged communication exists only where specifically defined in legal statute. While all states have some legal statutes defining privileged communication, the specifics of these statutes may vary from state to state, and the counselor has the responsibility to understand the extent of privileged communication in the state where she practices. Because privileged communication is the right of the client and not the counselor, the legal protection is valid only as long as the client does not waive the right. If a client waives the right of privileged communication, a counselor has no legal basis for refusing information solicited by the court.

HIPAA

The Health Insurance Portability and Accountability Act (HIPAA) is federal legislation enacted in 1996 to protect the confidentiality of personal health information (PHI) and improve the efficiency of its delivery by standardizing electronic transmission. The entire scope of HIPAA is broad and varies somewhat by service setting. However, the main practical requirement is that health care organizations are required by the Act to provide clients (or patients in medical settings) with a Notice of Privacy Practices (NPP). The NPP is used to inform clients how their PHI may be used and disclosed, and informs them of their rights to access that information.

Ethics and law

In counseling, ethics refers to standards and rules defining right and wrong behavior of the counselor. Ethics include not only what should and should not be done, but also, more on a continuum, what a counselor should strive to do and strive not to do. In practice, ethics are defined and enforced by professional associations such as the American Counseling Association (ACA). Because ethics are not law, enforcement is limited to judgments, by governing committees in an organization, that end or place restraints on the counselor's membership in the organization. In contrast, law is defined by government legislative bodies and judgments are made by the courts. Most laws governing counseling are defined by state legislatures.

Unethical behavior

Understanding and maintaining ethical practices in counseling is critical to a successful and lasting career in counseling. Recognizing common pitfalls in ethical practice will help to guide a counselor in the right direction. While potential ethics violations are many, some of the most common violations are:

- false representation of credentials, qualifications, or expertise
- practicing beyond one's professional competence, as determined by a governing ethics committee
- breaching confidentiality without a legally recognized exception
- sexual relations with a client; this prohibition continues for five

years after termination of counseling in the *American Counseling Association (ACA) Code of Ethics* (2005)
- negligence: the counselor did not follow commonly accepted standards of the profession and did not provide proper care to the client.

ACA Code of Ethics

The American Counselor Association (ACA) is the largest professional organization for counselors in the United States and the world. While its ethics code is oriented on its membership, it provides an excellent indication of the purposes of ethics codes throughout the profession. The main purposes of the *ACA Code of Ethics* (2005) are to:

1. clarify the nature of ethical responsibilities of ACA members.
2. support the mission of the ACA.Ethical behavior and best practices of ACA members.
3. provide a guide for ethical counseling practice that best serves the client and best promotes the values of the counseling profession.
4. provide a basis for processing and adjudicating ethical complaints and inquiries against ACA members.

While its ethics code is oriented on its membership, it provides an excellent indication of the areas addressed by ethics codes throughout the profession. The *ACA Code of Ethics* (2005) contains eight main sections that address the following eight major areas:

Section A: The Counseling Relationship
Section B: Confidentiality, Privileged Communication, and Privacy
Section C: Professional Responsibility

Section D: Relationships With Other Professionals

Section E: Evaluation, Assessment, and Interpretation

Section F: Supervision, Training, and Teaching

Section G: Research and Publication

Section H: Resolving Ethical Issues.

Suicide danger signs

One difficult ethical responsibility that counselors have is to recognize suicidal clients and make an effort to protect them from themselves. A key element of this responsibility is the competent recognition of known danger signs of possible suicidal intentions. Some of the most common of these signs are:

- previous suicide attempts
- verbal indications from the client; these may be attempts at attention seeking, but should be taken seriously and carefully considered
- client gives away valued possessions
- depression, especially severe clinical depression, is almost always present in suicide victims
- client describes a plan to commit suicide
- client indicates having the means (such as a gun or pills) to kill himself.

Role changes

When a counselor has a role change with a client, there is the possibility of harm to the client. Because of this, counselors need to do two things prior to making a role change: 1) carefully evaluate the possibility of harm to the client; and 2) obtain informed consent from the client. Three examples of role changes with possible ethical concerns suggested in the *American Counseling Association (ACA) Code of Ethics* (2005) are:

- changing from individual counseling to family or couples counseling, or vice versa
- changing from a counselor to a researcher, or vice versa
- changing from a counselor to a mediator, or vice versa.

Internet counseling

Internet counseling has many unique ethical and legal challenges that do not exist in traditional, in-person counseling practice. Some of the most common ethical concerns are:

- concerns of confidentiality due to possible access to client computers or email by unauthorized individuals such as family, friends, coworkers, and information technology (IT) administrators
- difficulty ascertaining whether electronic communication is from the client or an impostor
- possible compromise of unencrypted communications
- difficulty verifying that a client is legally capable of independent informed consent; the most common concern being minors misrepresenting themselves as legal adults
- discussing the possibility of technology failure with the client and providing alternative means of communication, should a failure occur
- misunderstandings due to a lack of nonverbal communication.

Mandatory and aspirational ethics

Mandatory ethics – Mandatory ethics are the basic, minimal standards of ethical conduct. This level of ethics is usually framed as things that must be done or must not be done. This level of ethics represents a sort of pass/fail criteria for ethical conduct. At this level, a counselor may be guided only by the desire to avoid legal trouble or professional censure.

Aspirational ethics – Aspirational ethics represent a higher level of ethics, going beyond the minimal mandatory ethics. In contrast to the pass/fail nature of mandatory ethics, aspirational ethics exist more on a continuum. At this level, counselors are driven by conscience and values to careful consideration of how they can best serve their clients.

Theoretical Approaches

Classical conditioning

Classical conditioning is one of the major concepts in the field of behavioral therapy. It is a process of learning in which an unconditioned response (UCR) to an unconditioned stimulus (UCS) is conditioned to be triggered by a conditioned stimulus (CS). The conditioned stimulus is associated in presentation with an unconditioned stimulus repeatedly until the normal unconditioned response to the unconditioned stimulus becomes a conditioned response (CR) to the conditioned stimulus. So, if you hear a bell every time you eat your favorite food, soon you'll be salivating at just the sound of the bell. The process was first identified by Russian physiologist Ivan Pavlov during his research on the digestion of dogs. Pavlov called dogs to eat food (UCS) with the sound of a metronome (CS). Eventually the dogs' normal response to food, salivation (UCR), became a conditioned response to hearing the metronome. Once conditioned, the dogs would salivate, without having been presented food, simply by clicking the metronome.

Solution-focused therapy

Solution-focused therapy has its origins in family systems therapy and was developed by Steve de Shazer and his wife, Insoo Berg. The key orientation of the therapy is its focus on possible solutions to problems, while giving little attention to why or how a problem came about. The therapy primarily uses questions to help the client "discover" solutions to problems. Typical questions: 1) try to find exceptions to a problem, focusing on exceptional times when things were working well or when the problem did not exist; 2) help define the client's goals for therapy; 3) identify changes that may have already been made prior to therapy; 4) place problems on a continuum (scaling questions) and help to identify partial changes or solutions to a problem; and 5) help the client identify ways to successfully deal or cope with a problem.

Cognitive distortions

Cognitive distortions—a major concept of cognitive therapy—are distortions or errors in reasoning that are present in one's beliefs. Some of the most common examples are dichotomous thinking, overgeneralization, and selective abstraction.

- In dichotomous (or "all-or-nothing") thinking, a person erroneously thinks of things categorically or in polar extremes, when they are actually on a continuum of many possibilities.
- Overgeneralization is when a person draws conclusions or makes personal rules based on limited negative occurrences. For example, a child falls off a bike on his first attempt at learning to ride and declares, "I'll never learn how to ride a bike!"
- Selective abstraction (or attention) is distorting perception by noticing only certain parts of one's experience. For example, blaming yourself for a failure, while ignoring your many successes.

Psychodynamic therapy

The four major theoretical approaches to psychodynamic therapy are drive theory, ego psychology, object relations psychology, and self psychology. All four are to some extent oriented on Sigmund Freud's conceptualization of three basic elements of personality: id, ego, and superego. In essence, the id is basic biological drives, the ego is rational thought, and the superego is personal conscience as influenced by parental and societal values.

- Drive theory is the original psychodynamic approach developed by Sigmund Freud, focusing primarily on the id and associated sexual and aggressive drives.
- Ego psychology is primarily focused on the ego and how through one's ego a person develops mental models of the world and how it works.
- Object relations psychology is focused on childhood relationships between a child and significant others (objects of relationship), especially mothers.
- Self psychology's primary focus is on love of self, asserting that self-love is an important element of healthy personal development.

Successful client change

Carl Rogers identified the following six conditions as necessary for change: 1) psychological contact; 2) incongruence; 3) congruence and genuineness; 4) unconditional positive regard or acceptance; 5) empathy; and 6) perception of empathy and acceptance.

- Psychological contact refers to the need for a meaningful relationship between two people.
- Incongruence is a client's psychological vulnerability or distress.
- Congruence and genuineness refer to the need for the counselor to be genuine, and the ability and willingness to honestly experience

and relate thoughts and feelings present in the relationship.
- Unconditional positive regard or acceptance means the counselor must accept and appreciate the client without condition.
- Empathy is the counselor's hearing and understanding the client's experience, with careful attention to the client's unique perception and personal semantics.
- Perception of empathy and acceptance means that beyond a counselor's intention of empathy, the client confidently perceives the counselor's understanding and acceptance of him.

Spiritual/holistic counseling

The biopsychosocial model of counseling refers to the interconnectedness of mind, body, and social context in consideration of one's mental health and general well-being. Many counselors also consider a spiritual component in this view of interconnectedness in human experience. While most counseling recognizes and considers this model of interconnectedness at some level, spiritual/holistic counseling is distinguished by a very deliberate attention to all of these components and their effects on mental health and general well-being. Holistic counseling gives much more attention to physical factors of mental health and well-being such as nutrition, exercise, breathing, massage, and others. Holistic counseling is also distinguished by greater attention to the spiritual component, considering such things as faith, meditation, prayer, and other spiritual practices and concerns.

Family systems concepts

Differentiation – The ability of a person to distinguish between her thoughts and feelings, and to be able to separate clearly her own thoughts and feelings from those of others.

Triangulation – When conflict or stress occurs between two people, a third person may be drawn into the conflict to reduce or redirect stress and anxiety. Dysfunction occurs when the third person becomes emotionally and relationally entangled in the conflict and the conflict is not resolved, but the entanglement provides artificial stability to the unresolved conflict.

Family projection process – The process by which one or both parents transmit fears, anxiety, and immaturity to their children. The degree to which the process occurs is significantly influenced by the level of differentiation of the child and the parents, with poorer differentiation leading to more likely or more intense projection to the next generation.

A-B-C theory

The A-B-C theory of personality is the core concept of Rational Emotive Behavior Therapy (REBT) developed by Albert Ellis. Each of the letters represents a specific component for understanding a client's experience and treatment. The theory also includes "D" and "E" components.

- A – Activating event: What happened and how the client perceives what happened.
- B – Beliefs: Rational and irrational beliefs, with therapeutic emphasis on irrational beliefs.
- C – Consequences: The feelings and behaviors resulting from the activating event.
- D – Disputing: Disputing irrational beliefs by detecting, discriminating, and debating the irrational beliefs.
- E – Effect: Rational thoughts replace the irrational beliefs.

In brief, a person responds to an activating event (A) based on personal belief(s) (B), yielding emotional and behavioral consequences (C). Damaging irrational beliefs (B) may be successfully disputed (D) and replaced with rational beliefs (B), resulting in new effects (E) in place of previous consequences (C).

Operant conditioning

Operant conditioning is a process of learning or training in which behavior is changed or trained through the systematic presentation or removal of rewards and consequences. Its basic forms are reinforcement, punishment, and extinction.

- There are two types of reinforcement: positive and negative. Positive reinforcement strengthens a behavior by providing a reward. Negative reinforcement strengthens a behavior by removing or stopping something unpleasant.
- There are two types of punishment: positive and negative. Positive punishment weakens a behavior by providing an unpleasant stimulus or experience. Negative punishment weakens a behavior by removing a pleasurable stimulus or reward.
- Extinction is the elimination of a behavior by removing any form of reinforcement.

Consciousness levels

Sigmund Freud conceptualized the human mind as having three levels of consciousness: conscious, preconscious, and unconscious. The conscious mind consists of all thoughts, emotions, and sensations that a person is aware of at the present time. The preconscious contains memories and information that are easily brought into the conscious mind and for which a person generally maintains a basic awareness. The unconscious mind consists of memories, thoughts, emotions, and motivations that are not easily brought into conscious thought. Freud believed that the elements of the unconscious mind were difficult to bring into awareness because of psychological resistance due to perceived threat or danger from those elements. A key therapeutic concept is the idea that the elements of the unconscious may sometimes be guiding or motivating dysfunctional or pathological behaviors.

Defense mechanisms

Defense mechanisms are primarily unconscious thoughts that distort or deny reality in an attempt to cope with anxiety-producing situations. While originally developed in psychoanalytic theory, the concept is now broadly accepted and applied. Seven types of defense mechanisms are:

- *Repression*: Repression is the most fundamental form of defense mechanism. It simply removes painful thoughts, feelings, and memories from conscious awareness. In essence, all other defense mechanisms involve repression at some level.
- *Denial*: A person simply refuses to accept the reality of a situation. Denial may involve thoughts, feelings, or observations.
- *Rationalization*: A person unconsciously develops "excuses" that sound true but are not, to justify difficult situations such as loss, failure, poor performance, and mistakes.
- *Projection*: A person attributes his own uncomfortable or unacceptable thoughts, feelings, or motivations to another person.
- *Reaction formation*: A person avoids dealing with difficult situations or desires by acting or behaving in a way opposite to his true desires and feelings.
- *Displacement*: A person redirects potentially upsetting words or behaviors towards a "safe" person, because directing them toward the true target is perceived as dangerous or threatening.
- *Intellectualization*: The anxiety of difficult emotional issues is avoided by focusing on the intellectual component of the matter and ignoring emotional content.

Psychosexual stages

Sigmund Freud, originator of psychoanalysis, believed that much of a person's personality is developed through five psychosexual stages of development: 1) oral stage; 2) anal stage; 3) phallic stage; 4) latency; and 5) genital stage.

1. *Oral stage* (birth–18 months): Pleasure is obtained through eating and sucking with the mouth. Emphasis is placed on dependency on the mother.
2. *Anal stage* (18 months–3 years): The anal area is thought to be the main source of pleasure through holding or passing feces.
3. *Phallic stage* (3–6 years): Main source of pleasure is now thought to be the touching of the genitals.
4. *Latency* (6–12 years or puberty): Focus moves away from pleasure and gratification to relationships, school, and other activities.
5. *Genital stage* (12 years or puberty–death): Focus returns to genital pleasure, but sexual energy is focused on members of

the opposite sex instead of self-pleasure.

Psychosocial stages

Erik Erikson conceptualized eight psychosocial stages of development related to life tasks that must be mastered for healthy development. Each stage, once arrived at, potentially remains throughout life, if not mastered. The eight stages are:

1. *Infancy: Trust vs. Mistrust*: An infant develops trust in his mother and others to meet basic needs. If needs are not met and trust is not developed, relational problems will result.
2. *Early Childhood: Autonomy vs. Shame and Doubt*: A child develops independence through potty training.
3. *Preschool Age: Initiative vs. Guilt*: A child deals with anger towards the same-sex parent and rivalry with the opposite-sex parent. The child learns through social and play activities. If the child is significantly denied these activities, guilt about taking personal initiative may develop.
4. *School Age: Industry vs. Inferiority*: A child begins to learn gender roles and basic school and life skills. Failure to learn these things may result in a sense of inferiority.
5. *Adolescence: Identity vs. Role Confusion*: An adolescent develops a sense of individual identity. Normal developmental tasks include setting education and career goals. Failure to successfully accomplish these tasks may result in *role confusion*.
6. *Young Adulthood: Intimacy vs. Isolation*: Vocational, social, and intimate relationships are developed. Failure to develop these relationships may lead to a sense of isolation.
7. *Middle Age: Generativity vs. Stagnation*: A person begins helping others develop and a sense of productivity and achievement is attained (*generativity*). Failure in this stage may lead to apathy (*stagnation*).
8. *Later Life: Integrity vs. Despair*: A person in later life (traditional retirement age) reflects on this life and accomplishments. When viewed favorably, a sense of integrity is enjoyed. If viewed with regret or remorse, he may have feelings of despair.

Free association

Free association is an assessment technique based in psychoanalysis that aims to draw important unconscious material into conscious awareness. The client is asked to simply state whatever he is aware of without any conscious censorship. The client is asked to report not only thoughts and memories, but also feelings and body sensations as well. Reporting everything in awareness, without exception, is emphasized. The client is encouraged not to withhold information even if it is uncomfortable, painful, silly, or embarrassing. The goal is to bring into awareness unconscious material that may be negatively affecting the client's thoughts, feelings, and behavior. Once this material is consciously recognized, the counselor and client can begin to address it, as appropriate.

Lifestyles

Alfred Adler believed that people are significantly defined by types of lifestyles. He believed that most people develop basic lifestyles early in life and are significantly guided throughout life by the lifestyle they have developed by about age 5. Lifestyles are significantly conceptualized by how a person approaches three major concerns of life: occupation, society, and love. Lifestyles are further understood in light of two key elements: *social interest* and *degree of activity*. Social interest refers to interest in relationships and social activities. Degree of activity refers to the amount of effort a person gives to dealing with problems of life.

Basic mistakes

Related to his concept of lifestyles, Alfred Adler saw people as forming *basic mistakes* in their style of life. These basic mistakes reflect errors in thinking or perception that negatively affect the person's thoughts, feelings, and behaviors. This concept shares similarities with concepts from other counseling theories, such as *cognitive distortions* and *defense mechanisms*. Two specific types of basic mistakes are:

- *Misperceptions of life and life's demands*: A person sees the demands or circumstances of life unrealistically. This may be reflected in statements such as "I never get a break," or "The 'system' is against me."
- *Overgeneralizations*: A person develops too generalized, all-inclusive, or all-exclusive views characterized by the use of words like *all, none, always, never, everyone,* and *no one.*

Spitting in the client's soup

Spitting in the client's soup is a counseling technique developed in Adlerian therapy. The technique is based on the practice of children at boarding schools who would get someone else's soup by spitting in it. A counselor uses this technique to help a client discontinue unhelpful or self-destructive behaviors. To do this, the counselor makes purposefully designed comments about the client's behavior that make the behavior seem less appropriate or desirable. The counselor does not tell the client that she cannot or should not continue the behavior, but merely attempts to change the client's motivations, so that she decides to stop the behavior without any direct suggestion. In fact, the client may not even be clearly aware that the counselor believes the behavior should be stopped.

Push-button technique

The push-button technique, developed by Harold Mosak, is used to show clients how emotion is connected to thought and to teach them control over their emotions. The technique involves three directed segments.

1. First, the counselor asks the client to think of a pleasant memory. The client is asked to make the memory as vivid as possible and dwell on it temporarily.
2. Next, the counselor asks the client to think of an unpleasant memory and gives similar direction.
3. Last, the counselor again asks the client to think of and dwell on a pleasant memory.

When this process is over, the counselor discusses the experience with the client and highlights the shift in emotion with each memory. If the client's feelings or mood shift as expected, the counselor emphasizes how the client was able to change his feelings or mood simply by changing what he was thinking about.

Prescribing the symptom

Prescribing the symptom is used to help a client develop a better awareness of a harmful or dysfunctional behavior, and ultimately to reduce or end the behavior. This approach is sometimes called *paradoxical intention*, and shares

- 45 -

similarities with a number of different paradoxical counseling techniques. In this technique, the counselor, without revealing his true intention, encourages the client to do the behavior more. The belief is that by doing the behavior more, the client will develop a greater and more sober awareness of its true nature and begin desiring to stop it. This approach may be particularly useful if the behavior is perceived as an attention-seeking behavior attempting to gain the attention of the counselor, because the counselor appears unconcerned by the behavior.

Existential therapy

Existential therapy is based in humanism and existential theory. While aspects of existential therapy vary among theorists, all are concerned with major themes like the meaning of life, free will, self-awareness, freedom, and personal potential. In consideration of the meaning of life, Viktor Frankl suggests that there are three ways people find meaning in life: 1) creativity; 2) experiences; and 3) change of attitude. Existentialists promote the *authenticity* of the client. The existential concept of authenticity is concerned with genuineness, self-awareness, and an understanding of one's limitations. Common goals of existential therapy are to foster personal responsibility, a deeper understanding of one's purpose and meaning, and increased self-awareness.

Gestalt therapy

Gestalt therapy, first originated by Fritz Perls, was originally developed from Gestalt psychology. The term *Gestalt* refers to a whole that consists of two or more identifiable parts. While Gestalt therapists find association with Gestalt psychology, Gestalt psychologists often disclaim any valid connection with Gestalt therapy. Gestalt therapy promotes awareness of self, others, and the environment. Gestalt therapy is also concerned with boundaries in relationships. The therapy focuses on personal responsibility, attention to personal semantics, verbal and nonverbal expression, awareness, and relational boundary conflicts. Four types of awareness are distinguished in Gestalt therapy: 1) awareness of sensations and actions; 2) awareness of emotional and physical feelings; 3) awareness of wants and desires; and 4) awareness of values. A primary goal of Gestalt therapy is the development of awareness.

Psychological needs

William Glasser, who developed a system of therapy called *reality therapy*, suggested that human beings have four basic psychological needs: belonging, power, freedom, and fun.

- *Belonging*: The need for belonging refers to the need to love, share, and cooperate with others.
- *Power*: The need for power and status is viewed as potentially problematic and often conflicting with other needs.
- *Freedom*: The need for freedom is viewed broadly, including such ideas as how we want to live, with whom we want relationships, freedom of faith and worship, and freedom of expression.
- *Fun*: While not as critical as the other three needs, the need for fun is still viewed as an important psychological need.

Cognitive schemas

The concept of *cognitive schemas* originated in cognitive therapy. Cognitive schemas are how a person views the world and reflects a person's fundamental beliefs and assumptions about life. There are two types of cognitive schemas: positive (adaptive) and negative

- 46 -

(maladaptive). Schemas are further defined by five distinct elements:

1. an affective component
2. the length of time a person has had the underlying beliefs
3. a consideration of the source of the schema
4. a cognitive component: how detailed and prevalent the schema is in a person's overall belief system
5. a behavioral component: how the person acts based on the schema.

Three-question technique

The *three-question technique* is a technique of cognitive therapy used to challenge negative or distorted thoughts. The three-question technique is a special form of *guided discovery*, another technique of cognitive therapy, which aims to help clients discover new ways of thinking by examining their thoughts in light of existing information. The three-question technique utilizes three successive open-ended questions to help the client better understand the distorted nature of his thinking. The three questions are:

- The evidence for that belief?
- How else could you look at the situation?
- The implications, if your belief is true?

Scaling technique

The *scaling* technique of cognitive therapy is used to challenge dichotomous thinking, sometimes also called categorical or all-or-nothing thinking. Dichotomous thinking is a cognitive distortion or thinking error in which a person sees something as existing in mutually exclusive categories—often as merely two mutually exclusive possibilities—when in reality the thing belongs on a continuum of many choices.

A counselor can use scaling to transform the categories or dichotomy into a continuum. An example would be a client who insists he must get a 4.0 in a class or he is stupid. The counselor can begin to examine with the client what it would mean if he got a 3.9 or a 3.8 in the class. By exploring and processing the reality of the continuum with the client, the counselor can slowly help the client see the significant distortion of the original "4.0 or stupid" dichotomy.

Social learning theory

Social learning theory is a major theory of behavioral therapy initially and primarily developed by Albert Bandura. Social learning is focused on understanding and explaining the learning that occurs in everyday life by observing others, or by what is modeled to us by others. The theory is based on three reciprocally interacting elements: personal cognitive factors, behaviors, and environment. Personal cognitive factors include beliefs, memories, perceptions, preferences, and predictions. Each of the three factors interacts with the other two. The theory also applies other general behavioral concepts such as reinforcement and punishment to explain how observation and modeling may be more or less likely to result in a learned behavior.

Observational learning

Four basic processes have been identified that help explain the ways in which observational learning works or does not work: attentional, retention, motor reproduction, and motivational processes:

- *Attentional processes*: The degree of focus or interest that is applied to observation.
- *Retention processes*: How well the observation is retained in the mind. Two types of memory

- 47 -

encoding are recognized in this function: *imaginal coding* and *verbal coding*.

- *Motor reproduction processes*: The ability of a person to reproduce the movement related to what has been observed.
- *Motivational processes*: An observed behavior will not continue over the long term unless it is reinforced (rewarded).

Self-Efficacy

Self-efficacy explains how a person's belief about his ability to do something can significantly affect his performance in that same thing. The concept refers to a person's sense of "I can" or "I can't" do something. A person with a high self-efficacy is guided favorably by images and thoughts of success. In contrast, the person with low self-efficacy is hindered by images and thoughts of failure. If self-efficacy is low enough, it may even prevent a person from attempting do something. To an extent, self-efficacy is behavioral theory's explanation of the self-fulfilling prophecy: first you believe it, then it happens. Albert Bandura identified four major sources that affected the development of self-efficacy: performance accomplishments (previous successes), verbal persuasion (encouragement and praise), lowering emotional arousal (reducing anxiety), and vicarious experiences.

Systematic desensitization therapy

Systematic desensitization therapy is used to treat clients who experience high anxiety or fear in response to specific situations, people, animals, or objects. The basis of the therapy is the development of *anxiety hierarchies* that identify various situations associated with varying levels of anxiety or fear. This hierarchy is sorted in rank order from lowest to highest level of anxiety or fear. The client is then taught relaxation techniques such as deep breathing or guided imagery to enable the pairing of relaxation with existing anxiety stimuli. Initially, the client is brought to a deep state of relaxation, and then the lowest-level anxiety-producing situation is introduced and sustained until the client remains comfortable and relaxed in the presence of the stimuli. Once this relaxation is achieved, the process is repeated with the next level on the hierarchy. As the process is repeated, eventually relaxation may be paired with the greatest anxiety-producing situation on the hierarchy.

REBT

Musts are a specific type of irrational thinking identified in Rational Emotive Behavior Therapy (REBT). As the name suggests, these irrational thoughts are centered on the use of word *must*. In brief, musts are distorted thoughts about what a person believes he or others "must" do. Three types of musts are distinguished in REBT: demands about self, demands about others, and demands about the world. Common examples of musts are:

- Things must happen the way I want them to.
- I must be liked and accepted by everyone.
- I must be competent and achieving in everything to be worthwhile.

Shaping

Shaping is a technique derived from the theory of *operant conditioning*, which is the broad theory of how behavior is shaped by controlling reinforcement or behavioral consequences. In shaping, behaviors that approximate the desired target behavior are reinforced, with closer and closer approximations being reinforced until a desired target behavior is achieved. Once a given level of approximation has been achieved, reinforcements are offered only for closer approximations to the desired target behavior. This process gradually encourages a movement towards the target behavior. For instance, a dad teaching his son to ride a bike initially offers praise for merely riding 20 feet and then falling over. Once this level of skill is clearly established, the dad does not continue to offer praise for this level of achievement, but only offers praise when closer approximations to skilled bike riding are displayed. This encourages the son to improve his skill.

Genograms

In family systems therapy, assessment of the family situation is a critical initial step. One of the most common tools used for family assessment is the genogram. Genograms are diagrams that graphically depict members of a person's family and their relationships to one another. A variety of basic information may also be included, such as ages, gender, key dates (e.g., marriages), medical conditions, mental illness, drug problems, and more. One of the key advantages of genograms is the ability to display relational information graphically, including such issues as conflict, enmeshment, disengagement, and separation. In general, counselors can include whatever information will make the graphic the most useful to them.

Family structure

Family structure is the core concept of structural family therapy developed by Salvador Minuchin. Family structure refers to the unwritten "rules" of how a family relates to one another. It describes patterns and expectations about how the various relationships of the family work. This structure is not something that family members consciously think about

and decide on, it is simply the natural product of relationship dynamics and expectations over time. Structure is best determined by actual observations of family interactions, which are more reliable than mere verbal reports. Structure is frequently changing as life changes, especially with changes in the members of the immediate household. Structure adjusts as babies are born, children leave the home, or family members die.

Family relationship boundaries

The relationships of family systems are partly governed by boundaries that affect the level of contact in a family. These boundaries can be seen on a continuum of interpersonal contact, with the middle of the continuum representing normal, healthy levels of contact—neither too close nor too distant. Boundaries that are more rigid and distant represent one end of the continuum, and may be called *disengaged*. Boundaries that are more loose and close represent another end of the continuum, and may be called *enmeshed*. At the more extreme end, disengaged boundaries can result in emotional and relational isolation. In contrast, highly enmeshed families, while close and supportive, may lead family members (especially children) to be uncomfortable by themselves and to struggle with social relationships outside the family.

Strategic family therapy

Strategic family therapy is an approach to family therapy that focuses on symptoms and problem solving. Goals are typically focused directly on the "presenting problem." The term strategic refers to the counselor developing strategies to solve the problem. These strategies may be direct and obvious with cooperative families who appear motivated and interested in change. With families who are resistant to the process and leery of change, the counselor may develop strategies that are purposefully indirect and subtle. In this latter approach, the counselor may be assigning paradoxical tasks that "trick" the family into positive change. Because the more indirect strategic approach is inherently manipulative, it is viewed unfavorably by some practitioners.

EFT

Emotionally focused therapy, developed by Susan Johnson and Les Greenberg, is a short-term therapy based significantly on attachment theory and structural family systems theory. While it is used for individual, couple, and family therapy, it is primarily used for couple therapy. EFT considers emotion as a foundational and primarily adaptive function, although the therapy certainly recognizes and seeks to understand maladaptive emotional responses. In EFT, the counselor functions as an "emotion coach," helping the client discover and understand emotional experience. The goals of therapy are to understand and reorganize emotional responses, change relational interactions, and increase relational bonding. Essentially, in EFT, emotion is both the focus and agent of change.

Family subsystems

Within the family system, different *family subsystems* exist based on such things as generation, gender, age, function, common interest, coalitions, and relational bonds. The two most universal family subsystems are parents and children. Subsystems have multiple and various subsystems within them. For instance, the children subsystem may have the following subsystems within it: girl children, boy children, teenagers, and non-teenagers. Less obvious subsystems (and sometimes more therapeutically important) are those subsystems based on function, coalitions, and relational bonds: for instance, a mother-daughter alliance, which serves to fight back against a verbally abusive father. The number and kind of family subsystems will vary significantly among families, and family members are a part of multiple subsystems with a different role in each one.

Narrative therapy

Narrative therapy, founded by Michael White, regards the client's experience as a "story." The therapy focuses on understanding a client's personal story, with careful attention to such concerns as personal interpretation and the meaning of language. Narrative therapy starts with trying to understand how the client understands her own experience or "story." Once the counselor understands the client's interpretation of experience, the counselor may then help the client explore alternative interpretations. The importance of different interpretations lies in the reality that our understanding of past experiences often influences our thoughts, emotions, and behaviors in the present and future. Narrative therapists attend to the meaning of language simply because our choice of words oftentimes significantly affects and restricts the meaning that can be taken from an experience.

Eclectic counseling

While many counselors are committed to the use of one particular system of counseling (or therapy), many choose to integrate techniques and ideas from multiple theories. This diverse theoretical approach is called eclecticism. Probably the most common form of eclecticism is the combination of cognitive and behavioral theory, commonly referred to as cognitive-behavioral therapy (CBT). Essentially, the combinations of theory and techniques are potentially unlimited, guided by the individual counselor's sense of what works for him. One challenge of eclectic counseling is that it may leave the counselor feeling disoriented, wondering what to do next in the counseling process. Similarly, without a clear theoretical orientation, the assessment process may also be vague and uncertain.

Solution-focused therapy

In general, solution-focused counselors use questions as the basis for assessment and therapeutic intervention. Three of the most basic types of questions in solution-focused therapy are: 1) *exception-finding questions*; 2) *scaling questions*; and 3) *the miracle question*.

- *Exception-finding questions*: These questions are designed to find out when the "problem" did not exist or occur, that is, the exceptional times when things were going right.
- *Scaling questions*: These questions attempt to create awareness of partial change in "the right direction." These questions are typically quantified, such as, "On a scale of one to ten, with one being the most depressed, how depressed were you last week and how depressed you are now?"
- *The miracle question*: This question is useful for determining client goals and guiding therapeutic direction. While phrasing may vary, the question is essentially this: "If you woke up tomorrow and by some miracle your problem was gone, how would you know?"

Decatastrophizing technique

A common cognitive distortion is catastrophizing: greatly or absurdly exaggerating a problem situation to the point of perceiving an impending catastrophe. One of the ways of addressing this thinking error is the use of the cognitive therapy technique of decatastrophizing. This technique uses "what if"-type questions to help the client gain perspective. Essentially, the therapist invites the client to consider what would really happen if the problem situation occurred, hopefully allowing her to begin seeing the exaggerated nature of her thinking. For example, a distressed teenage girl says, "Bobby must ask me to the prom or I'll die!" A counselor might respond by asking, "Let's suppose Bobby doesn't ask you to the prom. What will likely happen then?"

Attitudes

Carl Jung developed a concept for identifying personality types, which consisted of three dimensions on a continuum. One of the dimensions was *attitude*, with the two ends of the continuum being *extroversion* and *introversion*. This dimension of attitude refers to how people think about relationships and contact with other people. Extroverts tend to like being around other people. Introverts tend to like being by themselves or with few people. While these attitudes are opposite tendencies, they are not mutually exclusive. All people will have both tendencies, but for most people, one will be clearly more dominant than the other. The dominant tendency is a person's identified type of attitude, according to Jungian theory.

Functions

Carl Jung developed a concept for identifying personality types, which consisted of three dimensions on a continuum. Two of the dimension continuums were *functions*: *thinking–feeling* and *sensing–intuiting*. The thinking–feeling dimension identifies the way people make decisions or value judgments. Thinking types tend to rely on thought and reason for decisions and judgments. In contrast, feeling types tend to rely on feeling over thought in guiding them. The sensing–intuiting dimension identifies how people primarily perceive and respond to the world around them and themselves. Sensing types tend to rely on information from the five senses: seeing, hearing, touching, smelling, and tasting. In contrast, intuiting types, as the name suggests, tend to rely on intuition or "gut feeling" more than the five senses. All people will have tendencies on both ends of the two function dimensions. However, most will clearly have dominant tendencies on one end or the other.

Social and Cultural Foundations

Culture

Definitions for the term *culture* vary considerably, but some key dimensions of what defines culture are generally recognized. Understanding these dimensions is the best place to start in understanding what is generally meant by the word *culture*. The most commonly recognized dimensions are:

- race or ethnicity
- language
- faith, religion, or spiritual beliefs
- nationality
- gender
- age
- sexual orientation
- socioeconomic status (SES)
- marital status
- geographic location.

In its broadest sense, a unique culture is simply any group of people who identify with one another based on common characteristics, background, or beliefs. However, for practical purposes in everyday conversation and the counseling profession, the common elements defining cultures are usually one or more of the dimensions listed above.

Etic and emic

Multicultural counseling refers to counseling in which the client and counselor differ in some culturally significant way. However, there remains some disagreement in the counseling field as to how broadly the differences are defined and to what degree the differences must be considered in diagnosis and treatment. There are two basic viewpoints defining this issue: *etic* and *emic*. The etic view tends to define the differences more narrowly and sees the issues of counseling as essentially universal. The etic position does not give significant consideration to factors of culture in the decisions of assessment and treatment. The emic view tends to understand the differences more broadly and believes cultural factors significantly influence how the issues of counseling should be understood. The emic view believes that beliefs, values, and customs of culture greatly affect the issues of counseling and need to be carefully considered in assessment and treatment. For example, what might be considered depression in one person may not be viewed as depression in a person from a different culture.

Personal identity

Derald Wing Sue has proposed that personal identity can be understood on three levels: individual, group, and universal. The individual level refers to the basic elements that are unique to individual people: genetics and non-shared experiences. The group level refers to those experiences and characteristics that are shared by groups of people: race, ethnicity, language, faith, nationality, gender, age, sexual orientation, socioeconomic status (SES), marital status, and geographic location. These group characteristics are also commonly used to identify specific cultures. The universal level simply refers to our common humanness and those characteristics shared by all people: specifically, biological similarities, common experiences like birth and death, self-awareness, and the ability to use symbols and language.

Cultural encapsulation

Cultural encapsulation describes counselors who are removed from significant contact with other cultures and who tend to dismiss differences in culture and worldview. Key features or examples of cultural encapsulation are:

- seeing life and people only according to our own beliefs and values
- being insensitive to cultural differences and regarding our own view as the "right" view
- dismissing the significance of dependence and group identity in collectivist cultures
- disregarding the cultural context of relationships
- failing to recognize the cultural context of a client's social support system.

Alloplastic and autoplastic

There are essentially two major ways that people deal with the differences between themselves and their cultural situation. These different approaches to adapting are called *alloplastic* and *autoplastic*.

- *Alloplastic*: People attempt to change their cultural or social situation to meet their needs.
- *Autoplastic*: People attempt to change themselves to fit with their cultural or social situation.

How a counselor views these two different approaches is important because these varying orientations can lead to different goals and treatment plans for the same situation. Certainly, an exclusive commitment to one approach or the other is not necessary. It is possible that a counselor could address one situation from the autoplastic perspective and another from the alloplastic perspective. One might also address the same situation in part from both perspectives.

Ethnocentrism

Do not be confused by the root "ethno" in the term *ethnocentrism*. The term is concerned with all cultures, not just ethnicity. When a person defines and understands other cultures relative to his own, he is being ethnocentric. This does not refer to simply recognizing contrast, but to defining the contrast based on one's own culture. Essentially, ethnocentric people use their own culture as the "measuring stick" for other cultures. The view tends to assign primacy or superiority to one's own culture. In the counseling profession, some maintain the concern that counselor training, theory, and research are tainted by ethnocentric tendencies.

Individualism and collectivism

Individualism refers to the social perspective that the individual is of primary importance. It emphasizes self-reliance and autonomy. *Collectivism* refers to the social perspective that "the group" is of primary importance, not the individual. The group typically means a family, community, or society. In a collectivist culture, the needs and concerns of the group are considered more important than those of the individual. The dominant U.S. culture is individualistic. However, many minority subcultures exist within the U.S. that are collectivist in nature—the most significant being the various Asian-American cultures. Hispanic, Native-American, and African-American cultures are also collectivist, to a lesser extent. Recognition of this key difference in cultural thinking is important in counseling to avoid mischaracterizing the thoughts, feelings, or behaviors of a client whose views of the individual and group are different from your own.

Multicultural counseling competencies

The Association for Multicultural Counseling and Development (AMCD) has established standards for multicultural counseling competency. Section I of the standards is "Counselor Awareness of Own Cultural Values and Biases." The section contains three subsections; they are summarized below:
1. *Attitudes and Beliefs*: Culturally skilled counselors: 1) are aware of and sensitive to their own culture heritage; 2) are aware of how their own cultural background and experiences influence their thinking about counseling; 3) recognize the limits of their multicultural competency; and 4) are aware of personal discomfort with cultural differences between themselves and their clients.
2. *Knowledge*: Culturally skilled counselors: 1) understand their own cultural background and how it influences their thinking about counseling; 2) know how oppression, racism, discrimination, and stereotyping affect them both personally and as counselors; and 3) understand their own social impact on others.
3. *Skills*: Culturally skilled counselors: 1) seek education and consultation to improve their understanding of different cultures with which they are working; and 2) are constantly trying to understand their own cultural identity and are actively seeking a non-racist identity.

Section II of the standards is "Counselor Awareness of Client's Worldview." The section contains three subsections; they are summarized below:
1. *Attitudes and Beliefs*: Culturally skilled counselors: 1) are aware of their negative and positive emotional reactions to other racial and ethnic groups that affect the counseling relationship; and 2) are aware of stereotypes and preconceived notions they may have about other racial and ethnic groups.
2. *Knowledge*: Culturally skilled counselors: 1) possess specific knowledge about the specific group with which they are working; 2) understand how culture may affect a client's personality formation, vocational choices, psychological presentation, and help seeking behaviors—and, consequently, the appropriateness or inappropriateness of different counseling approaches; and 3) understand how sociopolitical influences may affect the life of minority groups.
3. *Skills*: Culturally skilled counselors: 1) should familiarize themselves with mental health research related to different culture groups; and 2) should pursue involvement with culture groups other than their own.

Section III of the standards is "Culturally Appropriate Intervention Strategies." The section contains three subsections; they are summarized below:
1. *Attitudes and Beliefs*: Culturally skilled counselors: 1) respect clients' religious and/or spiritual beliefs and values; 2) respect indigenous helping practices and community helping-giving networks; and 3) value bilingualism.
2. *Knowledge*: Culturally skilled counselors: 1) understand the general characteristics of counseling—culture-bound, class-bound, and language variables—and their potential conflict with various culture groups; 2) are aware of institutional barriers

keeping minorities from using mental health services; 3) understand potential bias in assessment instruments; 4) have knowledge of family structures, hierarchies, values, and beliefs of various cultures; and 5) should be aware of discriminatory practices that may affect their client population.

3. *Skills:* Culturally skilled counselors: 1) are able to engage in a variety of verbal and nonverbal helping responses; 2) can recognize institutional bias and discrimination, and protect their clients from inappropriately personalizing "problems" based in bias or discrimination; 3) are not averse to seeking consultation with the religious leaders and healers of client cultures; 4) conduct counseling in the language requested by their clients or make referrals; 5) have training in the use of traditional assessment and testing instruments; 6) should work to eliminate biases, prejudices, and discriminatory contexts in conducting evaluations and providing interventions; and 7) take responsibility for educating and orienting their clients to the counseling process.

Cultural formulation

The *Diagnostic and Statistical Manual of Mental Disorders* (DSM-IV, 2000) outlines a format for recording a "cultural formulation" of a client, which serves as a summarized reference of clinically important factors related to the client's cultural context. The format includes five sections, summarized below:

- *Cultural identity of the individual*: The counselor notes information about the client's cultural reference groups.
- *Cultural explanations of the individual's illness*: The counselor notes cultural language, terminology, meaning, and perceived causation related to symptoms, issues, or illness.
- *Cultural factors related to psychosocial environment and levels of functioning*: The counselor notes culturally relevant factors related to social stressors, social supports, and client functioning.
- *Cultural elements of the relationship between the individual and the clinician*: The counselor notes any clinically relevant differences between the client and herself.
- *Overall cultural assessment for diagnosis and care*: The counselor records a summary of all cultural factors influencing diagnosis and care.

Culture-bound syndromes

The *Diagnostic and Statistical Manual of Mental Disorders* (DSM-IV, 2000) contains a glossary of *culture-bound syndromes*, describing "recurrent, locality-specific patterns of aberrant behavior and troubling experience that may or may not be linked to a particular DSM-IV diagnostic category." In general, these "syndromes" are not commonly found in the United States, and when they do occur in the U.S., they are generally seen in people coming from a minority culture predominantly existing outside of the United States. For instance, an African immigrant reports problems that commonly occur in his tribal culture of origin and are identified as "illness" in that culture.

Proxemics

Proxemics is the study of personal and interpersonal space as it relates to the interactions between two or more people. In simple terms, proxemics is the study of the amount of distance people prefer to have between them and other people. Of course, this distance can vary somewhat from one person to the next. However, the preferred distance of interaction is generally consistent among different cultures. For instance, Latin-American, Asian, and African cultures tend to prefer a closer distance than do Euro-American cultures. The preferred distance also varies based on context. Four basic contexts that may be distinguished are intimate, personal (close friends and family), social (casual friends and acquaintances), and public. In counseling, attention to the issues of proxemics will guide the counselor in arranging the furniture in a counseling office and in his decisions regarding distance and posture in a counseling session. Poor choices, among other possibilities, might lead a client to misperceive a counselor as inappropriately intimate or cold and aloof.

Gender terms

Gender roles – Gender roles refer to the expectations of society for each gender. In general, expectations involve behaviors, dress, emotional display, and attitudes.
Transgender – Transgender refers to people whose gender identity or chosen gender behaviors are opposite of their biological gender.
Cisgender – Cisgender refers to people performing a gender role that is perceived as acceptable to society, but not necessarily what a person desires or feels comfortable with.
Androcentrism – Androcentrism means a person's worldview, thinking, and view of history are male-centered. In general, it is considered a form of distortion.

High and low context communication

The concept of high- and low-context communication, first proposed by Edward T. Hall, recognizes the varying degrees to which different cultures use situation and nonverbal context to communicate. In multicultural counseling, an informed understanding of high-low context differences can be important to avoiding miscommunication. In essence, some cultures are primarily oriented on the spoken word in interpreting the meaning of what is said. In contrast, other cultures significantly interpret what is said in the context of the existing situation and nonverbal content. Apart from cultural differences, the closeness and length of relationship also affect the degree to which context affects interpretation. For instance, families will generally have higher-context communication.

Mores, cultural norms, and statistical norms

A few terms that may often get confused are *mores*, *cultural norms*, and *statistical norms*. Mores are the customs, practices, beliefs, and attitudes of a particular society, especially as they relate to a sense of morality. As societies can include multiple distinct cultures, mores cross cultural boundaries. As mores informally indicate "right and wrong" behavior, they often have a significant influence on the behavior and thinking of individual members of society. Cultural norms are the expectations that a culture has for individual members of the culture. Cultural norms are similar to mores, but are exclusive to a specific culture. In contrast to cultural norms, statistical norms are measures of actual behavior among a sample considered representative of an identified group (which could be a specific culture), regardless of whether the behavior conforms to existing cultural norms or other standards.

Racial discrimination

A competent understanding of the issues related to racial discrimination is important for a counselor working with a client of a different race. Racial discrimination is treating a person differently and unfairly based on the person's race or ethnicity. Racial discrimination may involve something that is withheld or denied a person based on race, or something that is done to a person. Racial discrimination also includes the experience of a hostile environment—an environment that makes a person feel threatened, unaccepted, degraded, or harassed based on race. A classic example of racial discrimination is the person who is not hired because the employer is prejudiced against her race.

Religious discrimination

The U.S. has a very diverse religious and faith landscape. A competent counselor will need to have an awareness of the different religious beliefs of her client population and the potential experiences of religious discrimination. In essence, religious discrimination is treating a person differently and unfairly based on religion or faith. Religious discrimination may occur in at least three different ways:

- *Exclusion or denial*: Religious discrimination occurs when a person is excluded from participation or membership based on religion or faith, or when a person is denied something, especially rights or benefits, based on religion or faith.
- *Hostile environment*: Religious discrimination occurs when a person is made to feel threatened, unaccepted, degraded, or harassed based on religion or faith.
- *Coercion*: Religious discrimination occurs when a person is coerced by threat or pressure to practice or participate in religious activities or claim religious beliefs.

Acculturation

Acculturation is the process of change and adjustment when a person encounters a culture different from his own. Acculturation can be a difficult and confusing experience, especially for minorities in a dominant culture different from their own. Some of the possibly difficult or conflictual outcomes of minority acculturation to a dominant culture may be classified as follows:

- *Assimilation:* A person decides to give up the beliefs, practices, and customs of his initial culture and adopts those of the dominant culture.
- *Marginalization*: The conflict of cultures leads a person to reject her minority culture and the dominant culture, leading to isolation and marginalization in society.
- *Integration*: A person decides to adopt aspects of the dominant culture while retaining aspects of her minority culture.
- *Separation*: A person chooses not to make any changes or adaptation to the dominant culture, and fully retains his original minority culture identity.

Physical disabilitiies

Physical disabilities involve: 1) limited or difficult mobility; or 2) limited or no use of limbs. During their careers, most counselors will likely have some clients with physical disabilities. For those clients, a counselor should be aware of some special considerations of etiquette and courtesy:

- When the person is accompanied by someone else, be sure to address the disabled person directly, not through the accompanying individual.
- A person's wheelchair, cane, crutches, or similar aid is part of a person's personal space. Touching or leaning on these items may be considered rude or offensive.
- Do not pat a person with a physical disability on the head or back in a patronizing or condescending way.
- If it appears that the person may need some help, be sure to ask if she would like your help before giving it. If your offer for help is accepted, it is best to ask what specifically she would like you to do, instead of assuming.

Hearing impairment

During their careers, most counselors will have some clients who are deaf or have hearing impairment. For those clients, a counselor should be aware of some special considerations of etiquette and courtesy:

- If you need to get the person's attention, it is acceptable to tap them gently on the shoulder.
- Look directly at the person when speaking and do not cover your face and mouth; they may need to "read" your lips and facial expressions to understand you.

- If the person is being assisted by a sign-language interpreter or other assistant, speak directly to the person, not the interpreter.
- Speak in a normal tone of voice and use short, simple sentences.
- If a service animal (usually a dog) is being used, do not touch, play with, or otherwise distract the animal unless given explicit permission by the owner. Understand that the animal is working and distraction may interfere with the animal's assistance.

Vision impairment

During their careers, most counselors can expect to have clients who are blind or have significant vision loss. For those clients, a counselor should be aware of some special considerations of etiquette and courtesy:

- Be sure to identify yourself and others when greeting the person, and clearly announce when you are leaving.
- If the person appears to be in need of assistance or direction in moving, it is considerate to offer verbal direction or an arm to guide him. If using your arm to guide the person, simply walk with him; do not push or "steer" him.
- Offer verbal indications if you move while the person is speaking to you.
- If a service animal (usually a dog) is being used, do not touch, play with, or otherwise distract the animal unless given explicit permission by the owner. Understand that the animal is working and distraction may interfere with the animal's assistance.

Society and culture

Culture refers to a group of people sharing a common background, characteristics, beliefs, or customs. In contrast, a *society* is merely a group of people coexisting in the same geographic area or location, such as a country, region, state, town, neighborhood, or institution. The people of a society do not necessarily share a common culture, although they might; common geography can be a basis for a distinct culture. For example, the nation of Japan represents a distinct society and yet has a distinct national culture. It is normal for a society to contain many types of cultures within it. For example, the United States is a distinct society with numerous cultures: various ethnic cultures, regional cultures, age-defined cultures, and so forth. In essence, culture is based on commonality and society is based on shared location.

Kinesics

Kinesics is the study of how body movements are interpreted in communication. It includes consideration of gestures, facial expressions, eye contact, posture, and all other types of body movement, including unconscious body movement. Kinesics identifies not only what body movements mean, but also that a given body movement can have multiple meanings depending on one's cultural reference. Awareness of the latter is important for counselors doing multicultural counseling and trying to accurately communicate with clients from different cultures. For example, a typical white person in U.S. culture maintains eye contact most of the time when listening to others; a typical black person in U.S. culture does not maintain eye contact most of the time when listening. This difference in kinesics could cause an unaware white counselor to misperceive a black client as uninterested or rude when listening to the counselor.

Cognitive dissonance

The theory of *cognitive dissonance* suggests that people experience discomfort when two or more thoughts are in *dissonance* or not in agreement. The thoughts may be beliefs or attitudes, or they might be thoughts about one's own behavior. The theory suggests that when this disagreement occurs, people are motivated to develop agreement or *consonance* of their thoughts. Therefore, the theory provides one means by which a counselor can understand behavioral motivations and peculiarities. For example, a conflicted client who just lost his job may begin telling himself that the job really wasn't that good anyway and he was greatly underpaid, so it is really a good thing that he was let go.

Conflict models

Kurt Lewin developed three models of conflict: *approach-approach*, *avoidance-avoidance*, and *approach-avoidance*. Each model describes the nature of one of three different situations for goal-oriented decision making.

- *Approach-approach*: This model describes a decision between two desirable choices. This model is considered uniquely unstable, because approaching one choice tends to make that choice appear more attractive, leading to an ultimate decision for that choice.
- *Avoidance-avoidance*: Avoidance-avoidance describes a decision between two undesirable choices. This model suggests that movement towards one choice increases its perceived negativity and tends to increase the desire to avoid it, leading to more consideration of the alternative.
- *Approach-avoidance*: Approach-avoidance refers to a situation with only one goal. In this

situation, the choice is to do or not do something that has both desirable and undesirable elements. This kind of choice is usually the most difficult.

Interpersonal and intrapersonal abuse

All of the different types of abuse addressed by counselors can be categorized in two categories: *interpersonal* and *intrapersonal* abuse. Interpersonal abuse refers to abuse that is done towards or against someone else: it involves a perpetrator and a victim. Types of interpersonal abuse (which include some redundancy) are physical, sexual, emotional/verbal, child, elder, spouse, partner, and sibling abuse. In its broadest definition, child and elder neglect are also included as types of interpersonal abuse. Intrapersonal abuse refers to self-abuse or self-destructive behaviors. Most intrapersonal abuse is or can lead to some form of addiction. Examples of intrapersonal abuse include alcohol abuse and alcoholism, substance abuse and addiction, gambling, pornography addiction, overeating and food addiction, and workaholism (work addiction). In its broadest definition, substance abuse and addiction could include alcohol abuse and alcoholism, but often a distinction is made.

Substance abuse vs. addiction

Both substance abuse and substance addiction include not only the use of *illegal* substances, but also the misuse of *legal* substances, both prescription and non-prescription. Substance abuse is simply the self-destructive use of a substance, although the clinical definition of substance abuse from the *Diagnostic and Statistical Manual of Mental Disorders, 4*th ed. (DSM-IV, 2000) requires repeated use in a "maladaptive pattern." In either case, substance addiction differs with the presence of addiction-related patterns

and consequences. The most objectively discernable consequences of addiction are *tolerance* and *withdrawal*. Tolerance is the body's adjustment to the substance, causing: 1) a reduced effect or "high" from a given amount of the substance; or 2) a need for more to get the desired effect. Substance withdrawal is present when: 1) various withdrawal symptoms (e.g., a headache) occur; or 2) withdrawal symptoms can be reduced or eliminated by continued use of the substance.

Pit bulls and cobras

According to Neil Jacobson and John Gottman, there are two types of men who abuse women: *pit bulls* and *cobras*. Pit bulls are primarily driven to anger and violence by jealously and fear of abandonment. Like a stalker, they are constantly watching for, and almost expecting, betrayal from their wives or girlfriends. They typically appear normal and likeable to the people around them, but can explode into intense anger and violence when they perceive betrayal. Cobras are primarily motivated by the need to have things their own way. They are controllers, and their controlling behaviors are usually not limited to their wives or girlfriends. In contrast to pit bulls, they tend to be quieter and less openly affective until they become angry and violent.

Child physical abuse

Child physical abuse is intentional harm to a child, usually done in anger. While child physical abuse is more common with young children, the term *child* is not meant to be age restrictive and includes teenagers. Common forms are striking, shaking, burning, cutting, and throwing. Since abusing parents usually attempt to hide child abuse, it is important for counselors to recognize and be alert for common signs of physical abuse, such as:

- injuries in the shape of an object such as a belt buckle
- repeated injuries that are unexplained or unreasonably explained
- a child gives a different reason for an injury than a parent
- a child exhibits fear around parents and possibly other adults
- a child mimics abusive behavior when playing with dolls.

Child sexual abuse

Child sexual abuse is intentional harm to a child that is sexual in nature. As with other types of child abuse, child sexual abuse should be understood to include teenagers. Child sexual abuse includes not only sexual touching, intercourse, and oral sex, but also voyeurism, sexual remarks, and coercion to sexual posing, pictures, and games. Sexual abuse is much hidden in society for at least three reasons: 1) perpetrators do their best to hide their behaviors; 2) victims are frequently threatened and psychologically manipulated to maintain secrecy; and 3) much more than other types of abuse, victims are left feeling shameful and fearful of anyone finding out. Possible signs of sexual abuse that counselors should look for include:
- a child acts younger than his age
- difficulty eating or sleeping
- a child talks about or acts out sexual acts inconsistent with normal age-level behavior.

Child abuse vs. child neglect

While the exact legal definitions of child abuse and neglect vary by state, some basic characteristics and categorizations can be made. Child abuse occurs when a parent (or other adult) intentionally harms a child. Child abuse is typically categorized as physical, sexual, and emotional abuse. Additionally, the

exposure to or offering of drugs to a child is considered by some as another distinct category of child abuse. In contrast, child neglect occurs when a parent (or other responsible adult) fails to do something or provide something they reasonably should. Basic forms of child neglect include:
- Abandonment: A child is left alone. A typical situation involves a child being intentionally left at home alone.
- Physical neglect: a failure to provide basic needs like food and shelter.
- Emotional neglect: a failure to give adequate attention to or meet the emotional needs of a child.
- Medical neglect: a failure to provide necessary medical treatment.
- Educational neglect: a failure to educate a child.

Elder abuse and neglect

Elder abuse and elder neglect are increasingly being recognized as a problem in society and a concern in the counseling field. Some writers consider elder neglect a form of elder abuse, while others consider it a separate and distinct issue. Elder abuse refers to intentional mistreatment of the elderly, usually a dependent elder who requires assistance from other adults. The two primary concerns are physical and emotional abuse. Elder neglect refers to a dependent elder not receiving basic needs like food, clothing, shelter, and medicine. Not providing reasonable assistance with personal hygiene when needed is also a form of elder neglect. Elders, especially dependent elders, can be particularly vulnerable due to weakened physical condition and impaired or reduced mental functioning.

Emotional abuse

Emotional abuse is probably the most common form of abuse. It is common in both parent-child relationships and spouse-spouse (or partner-partner) relationships. Also recognized in counseling literature (although less commonly) is emotional abuse directed at dependent elders. Emotional abuse is often considered a synonym of verbal abuse. More accurately, verbal abuse is an element of emotional abuse, which also includes nonverbal behaviors like neglect and withholding affection. While difficult to clearly define and identify, emotional abuse is essentially words or behaviors that degrade or belittle others, often in a form of pattern behavior. The effects of emotional abuse are easier to identify than the abuse itself, and include long-term damage to self-identity and self-respect. It is probably more pernicious with children than adults because of the greater impressionability of children.

Stress

Stress is the physiological, psychological, and behavioral responses to stressors: difficult, challenging, or threatening elements of life. Stress responses include anxiety, muscle tension, headaches, worry, concentration problems, anger, increased heart rate, increased blood pressure, overeating, and difficulty sleeping. About half of all U.S. hospital admissions are stress-related, and approximately one fourth of all prescriptions written are for anti-anxiety medications. Approaches to treating stress in counseling include:

- cognitive restructuring: correcting cognitive distortions; changing patterns of thinking
- teaching coping skills
- teaching deep breathing and other relaxation techniques
- teaching and recommending exercise; may be assisted by referral to other professionals
- teaching and recommending changes in diet and nutrition; may be assisted by referral to other professionals
- teaching problem-solving strategies.

The body's physical response to stress is called *general adaptation syndrome* (GAS), which occurs in three sequential stages: alarm, adaption, and exhaustion.

1. Alarm: The alarm response is also sometimes called *fight-or-flight*. This is an almost instantaneous response by the body (and lasts only seconds), in which: 1) the nervous system produces epinephrine (also called adrenaline) and norepinephrine (also called noradrenaline); and 2) the adrenal cortex releases various stress hormones. This response prepares the body for action. Some of the most noticeable physiological changes include increased heart rate, increased blood pressure, and dilated pupils. The physical effects of this stage will remain long after its brief occurrence.
2. Adaptation: In the adaptation stage (also called resistance), if the stressor remains, the body begins to adapt and partially begins to relax. The initial feeling of panic begins to be replaced with reason and assessment.
3. Exhaustion: Eventually physical resources are depleted and the body can no longer maintain the response posture of the adaptation phase.

Career Development

Trait-and-factor theory

The trait-and-factor theory of career counseling is the first major theory of counseling beginning in the early 1900s with Frank Parsons. The basic idea of the theory is to identify a person's special traits and match them to the characteristics and requirements of specific occupations. The identification of traits may be done objectively with testing or more subjectively through interviewing and written questionnaires. Assessment of traits involves a consideration of personal experience, education, and background—specifically, identifying personal traits such as skills, abilities, aptitudes, occupational interests, limitations, and personal resources.

TWA

The theory of work adjustment (TWA) emphasizes the relationship and psychological variables of the person and his work environment. Its basic premise is that for a job to be a good match in the long term, there must be a congruence or harmony between the person and his work environment. Important considerations are job satisfaction, personal compensation, work location, work conditions, and employer needs. *Work adjustment* is the process of the worker and the employer finding and maintaining a working relationship that is satisfactory to both. Factors that promote the long-term interest of the worker and stability of the relationship—such as advancement, achievement, security, and social status—are called *reinforcers*.

Ginzberg theory

Eli Ginzberg, Sidney Axelrad, Sol Ginsburg, and John Herma developed the first theory of occupational choice organized from a developmental perspective. The Ginzberg theory is based on the assertion that career decision making is a process taking six or more years. The first phase begins in childhood and ends before age 11. The process ends in early adulthood sometime after age 17. The theory has three phases for this process: *fantasy*, *tentative*, and *realistic*:

1. *Fantasy* (ending before age 11): A child begins to think about what he wants to do "when he grows up." Play and imagination are sometimes oriented on work roles.
2. *Tentative* (ages 11–17): A young person begins recognizing personal interests, abilities, and values, and considers them in relation to career choices and requirements.
3. *Realistic* (age 17–early adulthood): A person narrows career choices and ultimately makes a decision.

Life-span, life-space approach

The life-span, life-space approach to career choice, developed by Donald Super, describes career choice as a developmental process occurring throughout life. According to Super, people develop their career maturity and self-concept through the accomplishment of five developmental tasks, while going through five vocational developmental stages: *growth*, *exploratory*, *establishment*, *maintenance*, and *decline*. The five developmental tasks are *crystallization*, *specification*, *implementation*, *stabilization*, and *consolidation*. The theory suggests that people partly select careers to provide full self-expression based on their self-concept. Developmental tasks describe the basic elements of exploring vocational possibilities, making career choices, making plans and goals, completing

- 64 -

training, beginning work, and establishing one's self in a career.

Vocational developmental stages

A key part of Donald Super's life-span, life-space approach to career choice is the five vocational developmental stages. These stages provide the structure for a process that begins at about age 14 and continues through life. These stages have a prototypical sequence but are not static. Life circumstances may cause a person to recycle through various stages; this is called a *minicycle.* The five stages are:

1. *Growth* (birth–age 15): Young people fantasize about different jobs. Interests, attitudes, abilities, and needs are formed.
2. *Exploration* (ages 15–24): A person begins to experience pressure to make a career decision. Choices are narrowed and an initial choice is made.
3. *Establishment* (ages 25–44): Establishment is a period of trial and stabilization. If initial career choices are not satisfying or otherwise acceptable, a person may make alternative career choices.
4. *Maintenance* (ages 45–64): A person is now fairly well established and begins shifting focus to maintaining and retaining career status.
5. *Decline* (age 65+): A person shifts focus to planning for retirement and eventually makes this transition.

Circumscription and compromise

Linda Gottfredson developed a theory, called Circumscription and Compromise, of how people become attracted to certain occupations, starting in childhood. Like Donald Super, Gottfredson believed that a person's self-concept is a key factor in one's career choices. Gottfredson

suggested that self-concept is primarily determined by level of intelligence, socioeconomic background, and developed concepts of gender roles. Based on these concepts, the theory includes four stages of individual development of occupational aspirations:

1. *Orientation to size and power* (ages 3–5): Initial views of work are very concrete and simplistic. Perception of self and others is largely based on size.
2. *Orientation to sex roles* (ages 6–8): Self-concept and view of work and others begin to be significantly based on gender-role perceptions.
3. *Orientation to social valuation* (ages 9–13): Self-concept and view of work and others begin to be significantly based on socioeconomic status perceptions.
4. *Orientation to the internal, unique self* (age 14+): Personal introspection refines self-concept and begins integrating concepts of self, gender role, and social class in consideration of career aspirations.

Typology approach

John Holland's typology approach is possibly the most influential and broadly applied theory in career counseling. Holland's approach to career counseling is rooted in the idea that people try to match their type of work with their type of personality. He proposed six different types of matching personality styles and work environments: *realistic, investigative, artistic, social, enterprising,* and *conventional* (RIASEC). Some people will find strong identification with primarily one type, while others will find more diverse identification with two or more types. Those who strongly fit just one type are considered *differentiated.* Those who do not strongly identify with any type, but more loosely identify with multiple types, are considered *undifferentiated*. Holland uses the term *congruence* to refer to individuals whose personalities closely match their job types. Identified personality types can be matched with similar occupations to guide career selection.

Personality styles and work environments

John Holland developed a theory of six different types of matching personality styles and work environments: *realistic, investigative, artistic, social, enterprising,* and *conventional* (RIASEC). Each of the six types relates to both a distinct personality style and a distinct type of work environment that fits that type of personality style, as shown below:

R – Realistic: Prefers concrete vs. abstract work; typically has mechanical abilities; likes tools.   Skilled trades: mechanic, carpenter, electrician; mechanical engineer, cook.

I – Investigative: Strong math and science orientation; task-oriented, analytical, and inventive.   Science-related fields: chemical engineer, surgeon, computer programmer, drafter.

A – Artistic: Values self-expression and creativity; enjoys many forms of art; likes intellectual work.   Architect, musician, author, designer, editor, advertising executive, artist.

S – Social: Friendly, helpful, likes social interaction; values service to others. Personnel manager, counselor, teacher, nurse, police officer.

E – Enterprising: Likes leadership roles; values success, status, and initiative.   Project director, business owner, manager, salesperson, urban planner.

C – Conventional: Practical, efficient, detail-oriented, and honest; values accuracy and order.   Administrative, clerical, and data work: teller, accountant, building inspector.

SDS

The *Self-Directed Search* (SDS) is a personality inventory based on John Holland's six personality and occupational types: *realistic, investigative, artistic, social, enterprising,* and *conventional* (RIASEC). The inventory assesses interests, competencies, preferred activities, occupational preferences, and other information that helps to determine the user's personality type. When the SDS is completed, a person is given a three-letter Holland code: for example, IRC, SAE, CEA, or RIS. The first letter represents the dominant personality type. The second and third letters represent the second and third most dominant personality types, respectively. This three-letter code can then be used to compare occupational codes that may suggest a good vocational match for the person. A benefit of the test is that it is self-administered and self-scored.

SCCT

Social Cognitive Career Theory (SCCT) is significantly based on general social cognitive theory and the work of Albert Bandura, including the key concept of *triadic reciprocal interactions*. The three elements of this interacting triad—personal cognitive factors (such as beliefs, memories, and perceptions), environment, and behavior—affect how a person learns and thinks about many things in life, including occupational considerations. Also important to SCCT is Bandura's concept of self-efficacy, which suggests that a person's perception of her ability to do something directly influences her inclination to try and level of achievement in the activity. Applied to career choice, self-efficacy suggests that both a person's career choice and success are affected by his perception of his abilities related to that career. The theory also draws on other behavioral theory concepts such as modeling and reinforcement to explain how career interest and self-efficacy are formed.

MBTI

The *Myers-Briggs Type Indicator* (MBTI) is a personality inventory based on four dimensions of personality from the theory of Carl Jung: extroversion–introversion (E–I), sensing–intuiting (S–N), thinking–feeling (T–F), and judging–perceiving (J–P). Each of the four dimensions represents a continuum of how people perceive, think about, interact with, and make judgments about people and life. The test determines which end of the continuum is dominant for each of the four continuums, and provides one of 16 possible four-letter codes for easy identification: for example, INTJ, ENFP, and ISTJ. The resultant four-letter code can compared with occupation listings based on the codes, indicating career choices that may be a good match for the personality type identified by the code.

LTCC

John Krumboltz's *Learning Theory of Career Counseling* (LTCC) is based on the idea that events and learning experiences of a person's life develop significant influences on career decision making. Four distinct factors are recognized as contributing to career choice: 1) genetic endowment; 2) environmental conditions and events; 3) learning experiences; and 4) developed task approach skills. Genetic endowment refers to personal qualities with which a person is born. People develop skills, interests, knowledge, and preferences largely as a result of environmental conditions and events they experience. Similarly, people develop occupational interests and attitudes based on a variety of learning experiences. Task approach skills refer to work habits, thought processes, values,

and problem-solving skills that a person has developed.

CBI

Sometimes a client will have beliefs and assumptions that inhibit or limit his ability to choose a career that best suits him. The *Career Beliefs Inventory* (CBI) can be used to identify these kinds of beliefs. The intent of the tool is to help clients and counselors identify hidden beliefs and identify new career possibilities that may suit the client. Generally, this tool is used at the beginning of or early in the counseling process. The CBI provides results for 25 scales organized in five categories:
- My Current Career Situation
- What Seems Necessary for My Happiness
- Factors That Influence My Decisions
- Changes I Am Willing to Make
- Effort I Am Willing to Initiate.

Strong interest inventory

The *Strong Interest Inventory* is a 291-item inventory that assess a person's interests to find good educational and career matches. Results are also provided for the following:
- 6 General Occupational Themes (GOT): level of interest based on Holland type codes—realistic, investigative, artistic, social, enterprising, and conventional (RIASEC)
- 30 Basic Interest Scales (BIS): examples are science, public speaking, sales, performing arts, mathematics, and athletics
- 244 Occupational Scales (OS): 122 for men, 122 for women
- 5 Personal Style Scales (PSS): learning, working, leadership, risk-taking, and team orientation.

OOH

The *Occupational Outlook Handbook* (OOH) is a career-information resource published by the Bureau of Labor Statistics (BLS), which is part of the U.S. Department of Labor. The resource provides detailed information on hundreds of different occupations and is updated every two years to keep the information current. The BLS estimates that the OOH covers about 88% of all jobs in the United States. The OOH is available in hard copy and online at bls.gov. Typical information provided includes a basic job description, work conditions, required training, earnings, and expected job prospects. The handbook also provides information about the current job market in each state.

16PF

The *Sixteen Personality Factor Questionnaire* (16PF) is a self-report instrument that measures 16 personality factors or dimensions. These dimensions have been identified through factor analysis as being universally applicable to people 16 years of age and older. The 16 factors are:
Warmth, Reasoning, Emotional Stability, Dominance, Liveliness, Rule-Consciousness, Social Boldness, Sensitivity, Vigilance, Abstractedness, Privateness, Apprehensiveness, Openness to Change, Self-Reliance, Perfectionism, Tension.
Test results are compared with occupational profiles based on the 16 factors, yielding unique vocational observations and occupational-fitness projections. Vocational observations provide insights into interpersonal skills, leadership potential, and academic training. Occupational fitness projections show the comparison of the individual's profile with established profiles for different occupations.

SIGI³

SIGI³ is a career-planning software program. It is the third generation of the *System of Integrated Guidance and Information* (SIGI), replacing the second-generation SIGI-Plus. SIGI³ is licensed for use by large organizations such as high schools, colleges and universities, libraries, military bases, and employment agencies. SIGI³ is designed to help the user identify work-related values, choose a degree major, and make career decisions. The system provides occupational searching based on values, skills, interests, personality, and both high school and college educational factors. The system also provides detailed occupational descriptions, educational requirements, and current wage and employment information.

O*NET

The *Occupation Information Network* (O*NET) is an online database and search tool produced in cooperation with the U.S. Department of Labor. It replaces the *Dictionary of Occupational Titles* (DOT), formerly published by the U.S. Department of Labor. The O*NET program serves as an alternative source of occupational information, supplemental to the *Occupational Outlook Handbook* (OOH). The database is continually updated by surveying workers in the identified occupations. The online site, onetcenter.org, provides four different search tools for finding occupational information:
- Find Occupations: search by word, phrase, titles, industry clusters, job zones (level of preparation required), career clusters, job families, and more.
- Skills Search: search based on 35 identified skills in six categories.
- Crosswalk Search: search by standard codes such as Standard

Occupational Classification (SOC) and Military Occupational Classification (MOC).

- Tools & Technology Search: search by associated tools and technology (e.g., lathe or Microsoft Word).

DISCOVER

DISCOVER is career-planning software licensed for use by large organizations such as high schools, colleges and universities, libraries, military bases, and employment agencies. The system provides assessment of career-related abilities, interests, and values. The system assists users with identifying personal strengths and needs and developing educational or career plans based on their personal profiles. The system contains a current database of occupations (including the military), college majors, educational institutions, and financial aid and scholarships. DISCOVER is organized by the following nine modules:
Beginning the career journey
Learning about the world of work
Learning about yourself
Finding occupations
Learning about occupations
Making educational choices
Planning next steps
Planning your career
Making transitions

Human Growth and Development

Biopsychosocial framework

The biopsychosocial framework is a foundational concept in human development, which asserts that human development is influenced by four main forces: biological forces, psychological forces, sociocultural forces, and life-cycle forces. Some redundancy exists among these four basic forces, which are explained in more detail below:

- Biological forces are the elements of genetics and human physiology, such as genes, prenatal development, and puberty.
- Psychological forces are the elements of thinking, emotion, perception, and personality.
- Sociocultural forces are the elements of society, culture, and relationships, such as family, friends, school, ethnicity, and community.
- Life-cycle forces refer to the importance of timing and context: how the same experience can affect people differently at different ages.

Piaget's theory of cognitive development

Schemas (alternatively called schemes) are the ideas or mental structures about life that children develop to organize experience and learning. Schemas are constantly changing with new experiences and children adapt schemas through *assimilation* or *accommodation*. Assimilation occurs when a child integrates information from new experiences with existing schemas. Accommodation occurs when a child modifies or replaces a schema based on new experiences. Piaget believed that all children attempt to maintain a balance between assimilation and accommodation. In other words, there must be both the application and the modification of previous understanding in response to new experiences. He called this process of balancing *equilibration*.

According to Piaget, cognitive development occurs in four sequential stages: 1) sensorimotor; 2) preoperational; 3) concrete operational; and 4) formal operational. The ages identified with each stage are only approximate. Actual ages of transition to the next stage will vary among children. The stages are as follows:

1. Sensorimotor (ages 0–2 years): Initially the child exhibits basic reflexive behaviors such as sucking and opening and closing fingers. Then the child begins refining intentional motor skills such as grasping and holding toys. Towards the end of this stage, the child begins to think symbolically, including talking, gesturing, and pretend play.
2. Preoperational (ages 2–6 or 7 years): Symbolic, pretend play becomes more common. Thinking is *egocentric*, meaning the child believes everyone sees and understands the world the way he does. Appearance is reality. Thinking is *irreversible*, meaning the child cannot apply reverse thinking or reasoning to something that is observed.
3. Concrete operational (ages 6 or 7–11 years): Children are now capable of well-organized, logical thought. However, thinking remains concrete: thinking about real, tangible things. Thinking is less egocentric and more reversible.
4. Formal operational (age 11+ years): A person begins to

demonstrate the ability to think in abstract or hypothetical terms. In addition to simple logic, a person now becomes capable of more complex logical thought: for example, if–then sequences.

Attachment theory

An attachment is an emotional and relational bond between two people. From a developmental perspective, the focus is on relationships in the first few years of life, especially infancy. The most critical relationship is the relationship with the mother. Attachment theorists believe the amount and kind of bonding a child receives in early life greatly affects relationships and emotional health later in life, including adulthood. According to the theory, the primary basis for good attachment is a mother who is present, responsive, warm, and caring. After an infant establishes a good bond with the mother, bonds with others are formed more easily.

The following terms are related to attachment theory:

Secure base – The mother or other caregiver provides the infant or small child with a sense of security that allows him to comfortably explore the world.

Proximity maintenance – Related to the concept of a secure base, an infant or small child will remain vigilantly aware of the mother's location and attempt to maintain a "safe" proximity. If the mother moves too far away, the child will become distressed, cry, and attempt to move closer to mom.

Separation distress – In early life, when the mother is still perceived as the secure base, a child may experience distress when separated from his mother. This is minimized by the formation of a strong, secure bond with the mother or other caregiver.

In attachment theory, four basic forms of attachment are recognized: *secure attachment, avoidant attachment, resistant attachment*, and *disorganized attachment*. Secure attachment is considered a healthy, stable attachment bond; in contrast, the other three are considered unhealthy and *insecure* attachments. They are summarized below:

- *Secure attachment*: A secure attachment is formed when a child consistently experiences a warm and responsive caregiver. The baby or small child is confident in the safety and dependability of the caregiver and is the least distressed when separated.

- *Avoidant attachment*: Children with an avoidant attachment appear unconcerned when separated from mother or other caregiver. When the caregiver returns, the child will often turn away or ignore the caregiver. This form of attachment may be caused, at least in part, by neglect or abuse.

- *Resistant attachment* (or *ambivalent*): A child with this type of attachment becomes very upset when the caregiver leaves and typically remains upset even after the caregiver returns.

- *Disorganized attachment* (or *disoriented*): A child with this type of attachment may appear confused or as possibly having mixed feelings towards the caregiver. For example, when a caregiver returns, the child may move closer to the caregiver but appear uninterested in her presence.

Information-processing theory

The information-processing theory of human development is primarily oriented on cognitive development. Information-processing theory uses the computer as a metaphor for the human mind. A computer has hardware and software. The hardware is the processor, memory, and input/output connections. The software is the programs used on the computer. Similarly, information-processing psychologists assert that the physical structures of the brain and nervous system are the mind's *mental hardware*, and the cognitive processes we learn and the information we store in our memory are the mind's *mental software*. Examples of cognitive processes include throwing a ball and adding numbers. You can add and upgrade both a computer's hardware and software, allowing the computer to do more and perform better. Similarly, in information-processing theory, cognitive development is explained by changes in the brain and nervous system (adding and upgrading hardware) and learning new cognitive processes and information (adding and upgrading software).

Gender awareness

There are three recognized stages in the development of gender awareness and understanding: *gender labeling*, *gender stability*, and *gender constancy*. The three stages are sequential, beginning with awareness at about age 2:

1. *Gender labeling* (by about age 2): Children understand that they are either boys or girls.
2. *Gender stability* (ages 2–4): Children begin to recognize that genders are stable: boys become men, girls become women. However, during this stage, children believe that behavior and choice affect gender. For instance, if a boy plays with dolls, he will become a girl.

Gender constancy (ages 4–7): In contrast to the stability stage, children now recognize that gender is permanent and does not change according to behavior or will.

The following terms relate to gender:
Gender stereotypes – Gender stereotypes are simply beliefs that people have about gender, regardless of whether they are true or not. Gender stereotypes are usually culturally normative.
Gender typing – As children grow, they observe and learn various traits, expectations, and roles about gender. Gender typing is the process by which children internalize these ideas about gender and begin to act accordingly.
Gender schema theory – According to this theory, as children observe life, they form an understanding of some behaviors, items, or activities as being specifically male or female. Subsequently, they will tend to ignore, avoid, or lose interest in those things that are associated with the opposite gender. For instance, if a girl decides "math is for boys," she may lose interest in math or decide she dislikes it on that basis.

Authoritarian and authoritative parenting

Psychologist Diana Baumrind identified four parenting styles based primarily on the dimensions of parental warmth and control: *authoritarian*, *authoritative*, *permissive*, and *uninvolved parenting*. They are described below:

- *Authoritarian parenting*: Authoritarian parents offer little warmth or nurturance while exercising a high level of control over their children. Explanations for rules are rarely given and a child's thoughts and wishes are rarely considered. These parents are not very responsive to their children. Children are typically obedient and capable, but also experience lower levels of social competence and self-esteem.

- *Authoritative parenting*: Like authoritarian parents, authoritative parents set and enforce rules consistently. However, in contrast to authoritarian parents, these parents also offer significant warmth, responsiveness, and relational connection to their children. Authoritative parents often explain rules and are sensitive to the child's concerns and wishes. This type of parenting tends to produce the most well-adjusted, happy, and successful children.
- *Permissive parenting* (or *indulgent parenting*): Permissive parents usually offer significant communication, warmth, and nurturance, but have few rules and rarely discipline. They generally have lower expectations for their children and convey few expectations to their children.
- *Uninvolved parenting*: Like permissive parents, uninvolved parents have few rules and discipline rarely. However, they also offer little warmth and relational connection. While they usually meet the basic physical needs of the child, they are unresponsive and uninvolved in their child's life. In extreme cases, there may even be neglect of some basic physical needs.

Adolescent identity formation terms

Adolescent egocentrism – The tendency for teenagers to believe that people are constantly focused on them.

Personal fable – Related to the concept of adolescent egocentrism, the personal fable is the tendency for teenagers to believe that their feelings and experiences are unique and no one can understand how they feel. This experience is typified by remarks like, "You just can't understand how I feel" and "Nobody understands what it's like."

Imaginary audience – An expansion of the concept of adolescent egocentrism, the imaginary audience refers to the experience of teenagers who feel that they are performing for others around them (their audience). This phenomenon, of course, can lead to a significant sense of pressure and stress for a teenager.

Intelligence

I In his *theory of multiple intelligences*, Howard Gardner proposed that there are seven different types of intelligence that reflect overall human intelligence: *linguistic, logical-mathematical, musical, spatial, body-kinesthetic, interpersonal,* and *intrapersonal intelligence*. They are described below:

- *Linguistic intelligence* refers to the ability to use language and understand the meaning of words. Linguistic intelligence is reflected in one's ability to speak, read, and write.
- *Logical-mathematical intelligence* refers to a number of related abilities, such as logical thinking, reasoning, mathematical operations, and analysis.
- *Musical intelligence* refers to a person's level of understanding and awareness of the various elements of music such as pitch, rhythm, and tone.
- *Spatial intelligence* refers to the ability to visualize and think about things spatially, including visual memory and graphical pattern awareness.

- *Body-kinesthetic intelligence* refers to the ability to move one's body, body coordination, and body awareness.
- *Interpersonal intelligence* refers to relational intelligence and awareness of others, especially with regard to such things as mood, feelings, motivations, and intentions.
- *Intrapersonal intelligence* refers to the degree of self-awareness—the ability to perceive and understand elements of self, such as motivations, emotions, strengths, and weaknesses.

Moral reasoning

Psychologist Lawrence Kohlberg developed a theory of how people develop moral reasoning. His theory suggests three developmental levels: *preconventional*, *conventional*, and *postconventional*. Each level is further divided into two stages for a total of six stages. In the first level, *preconventional*, moral reasoning is primarily guided by simple concepts of reward and punishment. The two stages of the preconventional level are:

Stage 1 – Obedience and punishment: Moral reasoning is focused on established authority and avoidance of punishment.

Stage 2 – Individualism and exchange: Children now recognize differing points of view and may begin to question authority. Moral reasoning is primarily guided by the anticipation of reward: "What's in it for me?"

The two stages of the conventional level are:

Stage 1 – Interpersonal relationships: Moral reasoning is primarily guided by the desire to meet the expectations of others, especially those who are close in relationship. Relational elements of empathy, love, and trust are important influences.

Stage 2 – Maintaining social order: Moral reasoning is primarily guided by a broader perspective of societal norms, roles, and law. People are motivated by the idea of being a good member of society.

The two stages of the postconventional level are:

Stage 1 – Social contract and individual rights: Moral reasoning is primarily guided by the idea of the social contract and properly established law, but concern is given to whether existing law is good and the possible need to change the law democratically. Greater recognition is given to varying values and beliefs in society.

Stage 2 – Universal principles: Moral reasoning is primarily guided by universal moral and ethical principles based on personal understanding, such as justice, equality, respect, and compassion. Moral reasoning in this stage is the most abstract.

Type A and type B personalities

Two different personality types have been identified in relation to how people deal with and experience stress. These personality types are known as Type A and Type B. Type A personalities tend to be very impatient, competitive, time-conscious, and aggressive. Secondarily, they also tend to experience more stress

- 74 -

and restlessness. In contrast, Type B people are easygoing and noncompetitive, and generally do not feel much urgency about things. They generally have much lower stress levels. In life, you might imagine a Type A person angrily honking his car horn, tightly gripping the steering wheel, and yelling at the carefree Type B person in front of him, who is driving too slowly in the passing lane and blocking traffic.

Personality traits

Modern research suggests that there are five major personality traits that apply to all people: *neuroticism*, *extraversion*, *openness to experience*, *agreeableness*, and *conscientiousness*. Each factor is essentially a dimension of personality on a continuum. They are summarized below:

- Neuroticism: People who show a high degree of neuroticism tend to be impulsive, anxious, depressed, hostile, vulnerable, and self-conscious. On the other end of the continuum are people who demonstrate more emotional stability and calmness.
- Extraversion: People who show a high degree of extraversion tend to be outgoing, assertive, and expressive. On the other end of the continuum (introversion) are people who are more reserved, quiet, and emotionally restrained.
- Openness to experience: People who show a high degree of openness to experience like variety and trying new things, and have a vivid imagination. On the other end of the continuum (more closed to experience) are people who tend to be uncreative, uncurious, and "down to earth."
- Agreeableness: People who show a high degree of agreeableness tend to work well with others and generally exhibit a caring and accepting attitude toward others.
- On the other end of the continuum (disagreeableness) are people who do not play nicely with others. They may be uncooperative and tend to be critical, antagonistic, stingy, and irritable.
- Conscientiousness: People who show a high degree of conscientiousness tend to be hard-working, persevering, self-disciplined, and dutiful. On the other end of the continuum (lack of conscientiousness) are people who tend to be lazy, negligent, and disorganized.

Hierarchy of needs

Abraham Maslow proposed a theory that people are motivated by a hierarchy of five fundamental needs, commonly referred to as Maslow's hierarchy of needs. The needs are usually represented as a pyramid, with the base representing the most basic physiological needs like food, water, and sleep. Progressing from the base, needs are increasingly more social and psychological. The highest-order need, at the top of the pyramid, is self-actualization, which refers to efforts for personal growth and the desire to achieve one's fullest individual potential. According to the theory, people will attempt to meet lower-order needs before attempting to satisfy higher-order needs.
Selfactualization-Achieve individual potential
Esteem-Self-esteem and esteem from others
Belongingness-Love, acceptance, belonging
Safety and Security needs-Shelter, protection
Physiological needs-food, water, sleep

Assessment and Appraisal Techniques

Reliability and validity

Two of the most important—and sometimes confused—concepts for understanding psychological tests are *reliability* and *validity*. Reliability refers to the accuracy, consistency, and dependability of a test. An assessment of reliability is concerned with the presence, kind, and degree of measurement error. Whether or not a test can be repeated and give similar results is an issue of reliability. In contrast, validity refers to whether a test is really measuring what it is supposed to measure. In other words, do the test results truly tell us what we think they do? For clarity, consider an extreme example: If we want to assess a child's knowledge of history and give him a test with math problems, the test results will not be valid because they do not adequately assess the child's knowledge of history. For a test to be meaningful and useable, it must be both valid and reliable.

Standardization and norms

To make test scores meaningful, there must be some reasonable standard by which they are evaluated or compared. Further, to ensure the reliability of the measure, there needs to be some defined standards for administering and scoring the test. *Standardization* refers to the process of establishing these standards. First, standard procedures are defined for test administration and scoring. Then the test is given to a sample population determined to be representative of the test's target population, which may be the general population. This standardization group is also called the normative group. The test scores of this normative group are the test's *norms*, which can be used as the standard for statistical comparison and evaluation of other scores in the test's target population.

Tests

An *intelligence test* is designed to measure a person's basic mental abilities: thinking and reasoning abilities. It essentially measures mental "power" and potential. While aptitude may be partially connected to intelligence, an *aptitude test* is designed to measure only a specific, narrow range of ability, such as a specific task or skill area. Some aptitude tests may cover multiple aptitudes. Aptitude tests are intended to assess individual potential in the specific target abilities. Possibly the most well-known aptitude test is the Scholastic Aptitude Test (SAT), which is commonly used to measure individual aptitudes in reading, mathematics, and writing. In contrast, an *achievement test* is simply an assessment of previously acquired knowledge and skill.

The following terms are related to testing:
Frequency distribution – A technique for systematically displaying test scores to show how frequently each score occurred. This distribution provides the basis for statistical evaluations such as *mean* and *standard deviation*.
Mean $(\overline{X})$ – The mathematical average of scores.
Standard deviation (σ) – A measure of variability or deviation from the mean in a set of scores. It is the square root of the average squared deviation around the mean, as shown below, where X represents individual scores and N is the total number of scores in the set:

$$\sigma = \sqrt{\frac{\Sigma(x-\bar{x})^2}{N}}$$

The standard deviation is the most commonly used measure for showing approximate deviation of a score relative to the average (or mean).

Standard normal distribution

The *standard normal distribution* is a standard bell-shaped statistical distribution based on the probability of distribution in random variation. The normal distribution curve is defined by two statistical quantities: mean and standard deviation. The mean defines the peak density of scores in the middle of the symmetrical distribution. The standard deviation defines the spread around the mean. Normal distributions provide a good reference point for understanding the significance of scores in a set. All normal distributions have the following characteristics:

- 68% of all scores are within one standard deviation of the mean.
- 95% of all scores are within two standard deviations of the mean.
- 99.7% of all scores are within three standard deviations of the mean.

Correlation

When two variables vary relative to each other, the relationship is called *correlation.* Although *nonlinear* correlation can be assessed, most of the time statistical correlation is referring to a *linear* relationship between two variables. If two variables, X and Y, have a *positive* correlation, when X gets bigger, Y also gets bigger; similarly, when X gets smaller, Y also gets smaller. If the two variables have a *negative* correlation, there is an inverse relationship: when one gets bigger, the other gets smaller. Mathematically, correlation is represented as a correlation coefficient equal to or between -1.0 and +1.0. A coefficient of 0 means there is no correlation. A coefficient of -1.0 or 1.0 means there is perfect correlation negatively or positively, respectively. A common error is to assume that correlation between two variables implies

causation. However, while causation may be present, it is not certain merely because there is correlation.

Likert format

The *Likert format* was developed by psychologist Rensis Likert for assessing a test subject's agreement or disagreement with a given item. This type of scale is widely used in personality and attitude tests. In a typical format, an item is presented such as "I like my mother." Then the respondent is asked to respond with the following five choices: strongly agree, agree, neutral, disagree, and strongly disagree. The choices can be worded differently or expanded to add additional nuance in the responses. In some cases, an alternate format with an even number of responses may be used to prevent the respondent from selecting a neutral response. The following six-choice scale is an example: strongly agree, agree, agree somewhat, disagree somewhat, disagree, and strongly disagree

Structured personality test and projective personality test

Personality tests are generally designed to assess different personal characteristics, such as patterns of behavior, ways of thinking, and personal tendencies—all of which may be identified as elements of individual personality. A *structured personality test* provides written questions with a restricted set of responses like True-or-False, multiple-choice, and scaled responses like "Agree," "Disagree," or "Don't Know." This objective test format allows the test to be standardized and statistically evaluated. In contrast, a *projective personality test* solicits subjective answers that are then evaluated subjectively. A test subject is asked to give a spontaneous, subjective response to a purposefully ambiguous stimulus. Projective tests are based on the idea that a person's interpretation of an ambiguous stimulus will reflect his individual thinking, emotions, xperiences, perspectives, and inclinations—and, consequently, may offer useful insights about the person. The prototypical example is the Rorschach inkblot test, in which the subject is asked to respond to ambiguous inkblot images..

Practice Test

Practice Questions

1. Which of the following men is credited with developing the field of counseling when he founded the Psychological Institute at the University of Leipzig?
    a. Sigmund Freud
    b. Wilhelm Wundt
    c. Carl Jung
    d. Alfred Adler

2. Who is considered the father of psychotherapy?
    a. Sigmund Freud
    b. Wilhelm Wundt
    c. Carl Jung
    d. Alfred Adler

3. Which of these statements best describes the relationship between counseling with psychotherapy?
    a. Counseling is more intensive than psychotherapy.
    b. Counseling and psychotherapy are the same.
    c. Counseling is less intensive than psychotherapy.
    d. Counseling does not require a medical degree but psychotherapy does.

4. What function is a counselor performing when she speaks with teachers about issues and factors associated with low socioeconomic status children and families?
    a. Supervision
    b. Training
    c. Consultation
    d. Organizational development

5. A. counselor who is ethnocentric would most likely need training for:
    a. Listening skills
    b. Cultural diversity skills
    c. Therapeutic techniques
    d. Ethics

6. An individual in the "integrity vs despair" phase of life, according to Erik Erikson is most likely in what age group?
    a. Infancy
    b. Adolescent
    c. Adulthood
    d. Elderly

Question 7 pertains to the following passage:

Susan has been feeling overwhelmed at home and at work. Six months ago, she had a baby and recently returned to work. However, since she has been at work she has been making more mistakes; her boss has to talk to her about this several times. She feels she may lose her job; however, the boss suggests she see a counselor to talk about the stressors in her life. Susan sees a male counselor in the community. After a few sessions, the counselor suggests she try to get more sleep so she can focus better at work. He also suggests that she take time for herself at home from time to time.

7. According to the passage, in what way is the counselor being insensitive to Susan's issues at work?
    a. He did not ask her if she now has more work.
    b. He suggested that getting more sleep and remaining focused is all she needs.
    c. He did not suggest she take more time off from work.
    d. He suggested she is not taking care of herself.

8. Which best describes the role of a counselor?
    a. To change people
    b. To give good advice
    c. To facilitate healing
    d. To solve people's problems

9. A counselor focusing on the unconscious would most likely use which therapeutic approach?
    a. Psychoanalytic therapy
    b. Existential therapy
    c. Person-centered therapy
    d. Behavior therapy

10. Which of the following best describes the therapeutic approach that focuses on how one thinks?
    a. Gestalt therapy
    b. Behavior therapy
    c. Cognitive behavior therapy
    d. Reality therapy

11. A counselor who reviews the rights and responsibilities of both the client and the counselor is practice what ethical standard?
    a. Confidentiality
    b. Release of information
    c. Informed consent
    d. Personal disclosure

12. What element of a group setting is present when the group moves from primary tension to secondary tension?
   a. Transition
   b. Conflict resolution
   c. Storming
   d. Informational power

13. Which of the following situations may make it necessary to break confidentiality and disclose information about a client to the proper authorities?
   a. A client tells the counselor he sell drugs
   b. A client tells the counselor she uses a fake I.D.
   c. A client tells the counselor he wants to harm himself or someone else
   d. A client stops taking medication

14. A clinician who is able to meet the different therapeutic needs of a wide range of clients probably practices what type of treatment system?
   a. Multicultural
   b. Eclectic
   c. Behavioral
   d. Multifaceted

Questions 15-17 pertain to the following passage:

The Smiths appeared to be a normal family upon entering family counseling. In order to gain a good sense of the family dynamics, the counselor spoke to each family member and gathered the following information:

Karen: 18 year old over-achiever with numerous full-ride scholarships to very good schools. This client is often found at home taking care of her younger brothers and sisters. When asked about her college and career plans, she stated she would probably stay local so she could remain at home. She noted she was happy with her life and felt she had a very good family.

Emily: 15 years old, very shy. Reports doing well in school; she is interested in the school drama team, but is too shy to try out. Emily keeps to herself at home and is often found in her room, at the library, or at the park alone.

Bryan: 12 years old, twin, involved in baseball and football, performs on average at school. Recently client has been getting in trouble at school for talking and being the class clown during reading and study periods. Family confirms "That's just Bryan, he's the family entertainment."

Ben: 12 year old twin, involved in baseball and basketball; however, unlike his brother, discipline is an issue. His grades are very poor, and he has had detention a number of times.

Mr. Smith: 56 year old businessman, works 60+ hours a week. He states he is home as much as possible but that work typically includes late nights and weekends. During this time, he prefers to relax with a cocktail and not be bothered by the children. He is currently upset over the poor behavior of his boys and feels it is his wife's fault for not disciplining them better.

- 81 -

Mrs. Smith: 55 year old housewife. She is very involved in the community and spends her days at community events and school meetings. She states that her community work is like a full time job and that it is necessary for the family to keep their upstanding place in the community.

15. According to a family therapy approach, which family member would be considered the scapegoat?
    a. Mr. Smith
    b. Ben
    c. Bryan
    d. Emily

16. How would Mr. and Mrs. Smith be classified in terms of their relationships with their children?
    a. Secure
    b. Avoidant
    c. Anxious
    d. Attached

17. What might a Structural Therapeutic approach suggest happen in this family in order to reorganize and foster healing?
    a. Mr. Smith works less.
    b. Karen does not live at home during college.
    c. Mrs. Smith gets her other children involved in her community work.
    d. Emily tries out for the drama team.

18. A counselor who assists a client with a Social Security application and helps the client talk to the Social Security Administration is performing what function of a counselor?
    a. Education
    b. Advocacy
    c. Supervision
    d. Consultation

19. What does a therapeutic group have that a support group does not?
    a. Specific rules for the group
    b. Weekly meetings
    c. Counselor
    d. Group leader

20. Which communication technique might a counselor use in order to encourage the client to expand on a point?
    a. "Umm-hmm" interjection
    b. Repetition of a word
    c. Restatement
    d. Paraphrase

21. Which of the following nonverbal cues may send the wrong idea to a client?
   a. Leaning forward
   b. Smiling
   c. Maintaining eye contact
   d. Wink

22. A client begins therapy with a new counselor. The client immediately tells the counselor he has been in jail for rape. After considering this situation, the counselor feels she cannot adequately counsel this individual based on her own prejudices. What should the counselor do in this situation?
   a. Cancel the individual as a client
   b. Continue counseling but do not talk about his crime
   c. Refer the client to another counselor
   d. Consult with the police

23. What has occurred when a counselor develops feelings for a client that go beyond the counseling relationship?
   a. Role reversal
   b. Transference
   c. Countertransference
   d. Psychodynamic shift

24. The ability for a counselor to communicate understanding and support builds the counseling relationships because the counselor is demonstrating what?
   a. Listening skills
   b. Ability to give advice
   c. Empathy
   d. Sympathy

25. What therapeutic approach suggests that an individual must compensate for physical inferiorities?
   a. Psychodynamic
   b. Gestalt
   c. Adlerian
   d. Existential

26. Which of the following therapeutic approaches relies on the client to set the course of therapy?
   a. Psychodynamic
   b. Gestalt
   c. Adlerian
   d. Existential

27. Which of the following concepts is most associated with Gestalt therapy?
   a. Teleology
   b. Principle of Similarity
   c. Daseinsanalysis
   d. Stimulus hunger

28. How does transactional analysis view the structure of personality?
    a. Id, ego, superego
    b. Working, visual, and auditory memory
    c. Parent, adult, and child
    d. Inferior, superior, and realistic

29. Which of the following techniques might a behavior therapist use to treat anxiety or psychosomatic pain?
    a. Systematic desensitization
    b. Modeling
    c. Positive reinforcement
    d. Relaxation training

30. With person-centered therapy, what must the counselor have that demonstrates authenticity and transparency?
    a. Unconditional positive regard
    b. Congruence
    c. Empathic understanding
    d. Internal frame of reference

31. What goal of RET therapy requires the client to question or challenge irrational beliefs?
    a. All-or-none
    b. Disputation
    c. Discounting
    d. Magnification

32. An individual with both a mental health diagnosis and a substance abuse diagnosis would be referred to as having which of the following?
    a. Co-Occurring Disorders
    b. Severe Disorder Syndrome
    c. Mental-Sub Abuse Disorders
    d. Histrionic Disorder

33. Which of the following is not a core social motive for entering into a relationship?
    a. Belonging
    b. Trusting
    c. Controlling
    d. Status

34. Which of the following theories would apply scientific principles to therapy?
    a. Development model
    b. Wellness model
    c. Medical model
    d. Intervention model

35. What is the educational requirement to become a National Certified Counselor?
    a. Associate's degree
    b. Bachelor's degree
    c. Master's degree
    d. PhD

36. The ideals of a profession are commonly referred to as which of the following?
    a. Professionalism
    b. Standards
    c. Criteria
    d. Best practices

37. Which of the following concepts leads to the "melting-pot" effect in an area?
    a. Assimilation
    b. Pluralism
    c. Multiculturalism
    d. Sociocultural transformation

38. Which of the following best describes the counseling terminology for the ability of a family to "bounce back" from problems?
    a. Strength
    b. Resilience
    c. Cohesiveness
    d. Determination

39. Which of the following refers to an assessment in which one score is compared to a standard score?
    a. Norm-referenced
    b. Criterion-referenced
    c. Standard-referenced
    d. Cultural-referenced

40. What is the most effect factor in being a good counselor?
    a. Knowledge of therapeutic approaches
    b. Good communication skills
    c. Personality
    d. Previous experience

41. According to Behaviorist theory, what type of learning requires associations with a stimulus and a reinforcer?
    a. Initiative
    b. Social learning
    c. Cognitive dissonance
    d. Classical conditioning

42. According to Erikson's stages of emotional development, when is the critical time for an individual to develop either initiative or guilt?
    a. Birth to 18 months
    b. 18 months to 3½ years
    c. 3 ½ years to 6 years
    d. 6 years to 12 years

43. According to cognitive-behavioral therapy, what can a child in the formal operational stage do that a child in the concrete operational stage most likely cannot?
    a. Think abstractly
    b. Think hypothetically
    c. Problem solve
    d. Use the senses to perceive the world

44. What is the average life expectancy of an individual who is diagnosed with AIDS?
    a. 1 year
    b. 5 years
    c. 10 years
    d. 15 years

45. Which of the following is not true about child abuse?
    a. Abuse can be physical, verbal, and emotional
    b. Child abuse occurs in all cultures and socioeconomic levels
    c. Abusers are often family members
    d. Abused children will abuse as adults

46. If following Erikson's stages of development, what might a counselor suggest to a client to develop generativity rather than stagnation?
    a. Volunteer
    b. Take a vacation
    c. Read a good book
    d. Join a support group

47. What does an assessment show when tested numerous times with the same results?
    a. Low reliability
    b. High reliability
    c. Low validity
    d. High validity

48. Which term refers to an assessment testing what it says it will test?
    a. Reliability
    b. Validity
    c. Analysis
    d. Concrete assessment

49. Which of the following is not a manner in which assessment results are used in counseling?
    a. Treatment planning
    b. Achieving goals
    c. Evaluating counseling
    d. Matching client with counselor

50. What type of assessment did David Wechsler develop?
    a. Personality
    b. Emotional stability
    c. Happiness
    d. Intelligence

Answer Key and Explanations

1. B: Wilhelm Wundt opened the Psychological Institute at the University of Leipzig in 1897. This institute was the first to give the field of psychology a means to systematically explore and test various human psychological traits. While Wundt is not the sole contributor to this field, his contribution radically moved the field of psychology and counseling forward. In fact, the field of counseling psychology dates back to ancient times when tribal chiefs would counsel individuals. Plato and Aristotle are also considered among the first philosophers to employ a systematic approach to examining the human mind.

2. A: Sigmund Freud is the father of psychotherapy. Based in Vienna, Freud made huge contributions to the field of counseling and psychotherapy. Freud believed that the unconscious motivated behavior, and developed the concept of the id, ego, and superego, advancing the theory that everything that people do and think is based on the dynamics between these three elements of the human mind. Freud is very well known throughout the world and concepts in the fields of education, values, and motivation are based on his work. Freud believed all human weaknesses were the result of earlier experiences, and often referred to childhood when counseling individuals.

3. C: Counseling is widely considered to be less intensive than psychotherapy. The main goal in counseling is preventative and is typically accomplished in few sessions. Other goals of counseling include education, problem solving, and support. On the other hand, psychotherapy is typically of longer duration and has the goal of intervention. The settings in which these two types of therapy also vary. Counseling typically occurs in schools and businesses, while psychotherapy is more often conducted in hospitals or mental health centers. While these differences do exist between the two therapies, overlap is becoming more common. In general, the type and intensity of the therapy should be determined by the needs of the client.

4. C: Consultation is one function of today's counselors. Also called "indirect helping," consultation is a way to reach populations that might not otherwise seek out services. This is particularly important in schools because teachers consulting with counselors can learn about different techniques or services available to help their students. Other functions of counselors include training, supervision, and organizational development. In terms of training, a counselor may provide individual or group sessions focused on time management, problem solving, or anger management. These issues do not only stem from psychological problems; they can be caused by a lack of knowledge about how to better handle situations requiring these skills. Supervision is important in helping new counselors develop best practices and seeking help with difficult cases. Finally, organizational development is when a counselor enters organizations to offer services on behalf of employees or the organization itself.

5. B: By definition, ethnocentric means feeling that one's own culture is superior to others. Counselors work with many people from various cultures. It is important to maintain a clear understanding of one's own culture as well as of other cultures in order to effectively treat clients. Culture plays a very important role in how both therapist and client view the counseling relationship, and their ultimate success in counseling. Counselors who are multiculturally skilled will have deeper understandings of their clients' home cultures, values, and beliefs, and will be sensitive to differences between cultures and recognize their own biases.

6. D: An individual in the integrity vs. despair phase is, according to Erik Erikson, most likely elderly. There are special considerations in the counseling environment for this population that all counselors must understand and respect. Erikson defines this population as facing either integrity or despair because of the crossroads at which these clients find themselves. The elderly have many experiences and have, over the years, acquired wisdom. However, they may also feel less useful to the community and their families. Those living in nursing homes or dealing with various health issues may not be able to care for themselves and often experience feelings of depression and worthlessness.

7. B: Men and women react differently to different situations. Additionally, men may not fully understand the stressors women face. In this situation, the counselor suggested Susan gets more sleep to stay focused at work. Essentially, he is suggesting that she adapt her lifestyle to her current work situation. Historically, counseling has focused on a male process; male counselors often suggest women clients need to simply adapt or adjust. A. successful counselor, male or female, will understand that there are significant gender differences that must be treated with sensitivity in the counseling environment.

8. C: The role of the counselor is to facilitate healing. This is done through discussion and the use of various therapeutic techniques. However, a good counselor must also have a deep understanding of human nature and be able to practice empathy. A. counselor will help clients explore their lives and problems in ways clients may not have thought of before. Counselors may also teach various skills in problem solving and decision making. The counselor will not make decisions for clients, but rather assist in the process and provide support so clients can learn how to make their own decisions and solve their own problems.

9. A: Psychoanalytic therapy focuses on the unconscious. This therapeutic approach was developed by Sigmund Freud and suggests that it is the unconscious that motivates and dictates behavior, and looks to early childhood where personal development occurs for the origin. The structures of this approach, which lie in the unconscious, include the id, ego, and superego. The id, according to Freud, is the first personality; there is no organization with this structure and the id is motivated by pleasure. The ego is the controlling structure of the personality which is not formed at birth; however, it is later developed to act as a censor between the id and outside world. The superego is responsible for values and morals.

10. C: Cognitive behavior therapy focuses on cognition, or thoughts about actions and behaviors. Cognitive therapy was founded by Albert Ellis, who felt that people can have either straight, rational, thinking patterns or crooked, irrational thinking

patterns. Maladaptive behavior patterns are the result of irrational thinking. Cognitive behavioral therapy works to teach clients how to rethink irrational thoughts and apply them to their behaviors. This therapeutic approach typically follows an A-B-C framework. Using this framework, the counselor and clients identify the event that led to irrational thoughts, emotional disturbance or maladaptive behaviors. Once this is identified, the intervention proceeds and the client learns how to alter thinking from the irrational to the rational.

11. C: One ethical standard of the American Counseling Association is to provide all clients with informed consent in writing and presented verbally. It provides clients with information about the counseling process. Ethically responsible counselors will provide this information to their clients because all clients have the right to know about the counseling relationship and make an informed decision to engage in such a relationship. For those counselors working with minors, informed consent must also be provided to the legal guardians of the client. Included in the informed consent will be information on confidentiality as well as a detailed outline of the role of the counselor. Additionally, all discussions that are included in the informed consent must be documented.

12. C: When the group setting moves from a primary to a secondary tension, storming occurs. In the group setting, feeling uncomfortable due to a new situation defines primary tension. As members of the group becomes more comfortable with one another, secondary tension sets in and may result in conflicts within the group. During this process, it will be important for group members to clearly and openly express themselves in order to relieve the tension, in turn helping the healing environment and goals of the group.

13. C: Confidentiality is important in the counseling field. However, there may be times where it is necessary to break confidentiality. If a client informs a counselor of the desire to harm himself or someone else, it may be necessary to alert authorities. Breaking confidentiality is also warranted where child abuse is suspected, the client may need to be hospitalized, or the client simply requests that information be released. In any case, the counselor must ensure that the proper steps for releasing information be taken, including full documentation of the release of records.

14. B: Taking an eclectic approach to the counseling relationship is beneficial because not all approaches are appropriate for a particular client and there are numerous therapeutic approaches available. There are four main types of eclecticism. Theoretical eclecticism focuses on development; common factors eclecticism focuses on support from the community and family; technical eclecticism borrows from the many theories available and applies them to the treatment plan; and theoretical integration is a specific guideline developed for clinicians to provide the best care possible to their clients.

15. B: In this case, Ben is the scapegoat. While the family's specific issues are unclear, it is obvious that Ben is the family member who has assumed the burden of acting out, with poor grades and disciplinary problems. This classification is often seen in families with one or more alcoholic members; it is scapegoats who tend to feel the brunt of the dysfunction. Family members join together to give the impression all is well in the family itself except for the problems of the scapegoat.

16. B: Mr. and Mrs. Smith's relationship with their children is avoidant. In this type of relationship the individuals involved do not feel comfortable being around each other. Based on an initial assessment, it appears that both parents spend more time outside the home working or doing community work than they do at home. Karen's comments about staying close to home in order to take care of the family despite her ability to go away for school indicates that she doesn't feel her parents take care of the other children sufficiently. In addition, the twins' behavioral problems are likely a cry for the attention that they are not receiving at home.

17. B: The main focus of Structural Therapy is to first create disorganization and disequilibrium within the family in order to permit the family to reorganize in a more positive way, shedding their dysfunctional roles in the process. Based on the information given, it is clear that the parents in this family prefer to be away from the home, leaving the children to fend for themselves or be taken care of by the eldest daughter, Karen. If Karen were to go away for college it would create disequilibrium, forcing the other family members to react as well. The children still in the home would need someone to care and cook for them. This, along with other suggestions, may cause the parents to spend more time at home, giving the children and family as a whole the support and attention they need.

18. B: Advocacy is one of the functions of the counselor. The exact duties of this function vary depending on the needs of the clients; they may range from helping them speak to the Social Security Administration, to speaking for them in court. Those counselors who serve minors may also need to advocate for their clients for educational services. Since this is one of the functions of a counselor, it is important to be aware of the various services available as well as of other professionals in the community that might benefit your clients.

19. C: Therapeutic groups include a professional counselor, while support groups will not. There will, however, typically be a group leader who is a member of the support group or familiar with its experiences. Other differences include the goals and focus of each type of group. Therapeutic groups focus on change by means of therapy. On the other hand, a support group's focus will be solely on support of the members. Members of support groups find that it helps the healing process to have a place to talk with others about problems they are all facing.

20. B: While the client is talking it is important for the counselor to be actively listening; this can be accomplished in a number of ways. If the counselor would like the client to expand on a topic or statement, repeating a word the client said in the form of a question is effective. This strategy forces the client to refocus on the word and prompts him to expand. Other techniques for active listening include the "umm-hmm" interjection. This technique is a quick interjection which tells the client you are listening and understand what is being spoken. Restatements can also be used to focus the client on one specific point he has just made. Paraphrasing can be used once the client has finished and allows the counselor to clarify what was said.

21. D: A wink may send the wrong idea to a client. Nonverbal communication can say as much as verbal communication; it's important for counselors to be aware of how gestures and other cues might be interpreted. Good counselors will maintain

good eye contact, smile, nod, and lean forward. This will tell the client that the counselor is listening. Counselors can also observe their clients' nonverbal cues to determine how they may be feeling. If a client enters with slumped shoulders or crosses her arms crossed upon sitting, the counselor will see by the body language that something is wrong.

22. C: There may be clients that a counselor cannot adequately help for a variety of reasons. In these cases, the professional thing to do is to refer that client to someone who may be better equipped to do so. Unwillingness to refer a client when needed may result in harmful outcomes for either the client of the counselor.

23. C: Countertransference occurs when a counselor develops feelings for a client that go beyond the counseling relationship. This phenomenon was discussed by Freud. The effects of countertransference vary, however they often take the shape of the counselor becoming involved in the client's life to the point of taking on the client's issues and problems. To avoid this occurrence, it is important to set up clear client-counselor boundaries. By developing clear boundaries, counselor and clients will be well aware of where the counseling relationship begins and ends.

24. C: Relationship building is key in the counseling relationship. As the relationship builds and trust increases, the client is willing to disclose more information, thus helping the healing process. Empathy is one aspect of this process. In the counseling relationship displaying empathy is a two-step process. First, empathy is demonstrated by understanding. The counselor can do this by paraphrasing what the client has said to confirm understanding. In the second step, the counselor can verbally acknowledge unspoken thoughts or feelings the client has expressed nonverbally.

25. C: Adlerian therapy is a therapeutic approach that suggests an individual must compensate for physical inferiorities. Because of these feelings of inferiority, individuals aim to reach superiority, which serves as a main motivator. Rather than looking to the past to uncover emotional disturbances, this therapeutic approach looks to the future as the individual attempts to reach finalism. In reaching finalism, the individuals have reached perfection. This is accomplished through the development of goals. It is when an individual struggles to reach or overcome his inferiority that maladaptive behaviors form, also referred to as inferiority complexes. Using this therapeutic approach, it is the counselor's role to provide clients with education and encouragement in order to help them overcome their inferiorities.

26. D: Existential therapy relies on the client to set the course for the therapy. It is the role of the therapist to simply provide advocacy and support to the client. This therapy differs from other types because there is no focus placed on the unconscious as a means for maladaptive behavior. Rather, maladaptive behavior is developed by not taking responsibility for actions and not being self-aware; developing self-awareness and taking responsibility for actions and their outcomes will induce change and healing.

27. B: The principle of similarity is associated with Gestalt therapy. This therapeutic approach looks at the world as a whole made up of smaller parts. The principle of

similarity refers to the tendency of individuals to group things that are similar. Likewise, the principle of closure is the tendency to fill in missing pieces in order to comprehend the whole picture or situation. The third principle of this therapeutic approach is that of proximity. The principle of proximity is the tendency to group things according to how close in distance they are to other objects.

28. B: Transactional analysis views the structure of personality as being composed of the parent, adult, and the child. The parent ego is composed of thoughts and memories of how adults treated the client as a child. From this comes the nurturing parent who is supportive and loving or the critical parent who is rejecting and judgmental. The child ego holds uninhibited psychic energy that must be controlled. It is the adult ego that controls and monitors the parent and the child egos.

29. D: Relaxation training is used by behavioral therapists for a number of conditions including psychosomatic pain and anxiety. With this training, the therapist teaches the client to relax muscle groups one by one until complete relaxation has occurred. The therapist will begin with one muscle group and speak in soft tones until the client can relax the target muscles, then moves to the next group of muscles. While some clients may be able to fully relax during one session, other may require a number of sessions to learn the technique

30. B: Congruence describes an individual who is genuine and transparent. Person-centered therapy sees this as an essential quality in the counselor in order that clients can establish trust. With this therapeutic approach it is acceptable for the counselor to show feelings; however, he should not disclose information that is not relevant to the client's discussion. For example, it would be appropriate to share feelings of sadness if the client tells the counselor about a sad situation, but inappropriate for the counselor to disclose a sad personal story of his own during the counseling session.

31. B: Disputation is the therapeutic method of challenging irrational beliefs. This process will occur in the second stage of RET therapy, where the client seeks a more rational way to think. In the therapy session a client will be required to provide rational evidence for irrational beliefs. There are three types of disputations; cognitive, imaginal, and behavioral. With cognitive disputations, the client is asked a series of questions about the reality of the irrational belief. With imaginal disputation, the client images a situation in which irrational thoughts appear and are guided to rethink the situation using rational thoughts. With behavioral disputations, the client is required to change behaviors and thus change their irrational beliefs.

32. A: Co-occurring disorders is the term used when an individual has both a mental health and a substance diagnosis. Counselors must be aware of clients with co-occurring disorders for a number of reasons. First, the individual may be receiving treatment for each from two different counselors. In these cases, the counselors should communicate in order to provide the client with consistent and effective treatment. A second factor is medication for one or both diagnosis. Treating co-occurring disorders can be tricky because one disorder could be related to the other. For example and individual may be depressed and drinks to self-medicate, but the drinking causes the depression to worsen.

33. D: While status may be gained by entering into a relationship, it is not considered a core social motive for doing so. However, feelings of belonging, trust and control are universal social motives. Belonging refers to an individual's social need to be a part of something. As the individual grows this need expands from the family to the community and on to a more global sense of belonging. Trust is a motive because it brings about consistency and predictability in relationships, which in turn provides security. Control works in conjunction with trust to provide security within a relationship.

34. C: The medical model uses scientific principles when applying therapeutic interventions. With this model the practitioner conducts a thorough assessment of the client and then develops a treatment plan. Medical models often rely on the use of medications in their treatment plans. The main goal of the medical model is to bring the client back to the same functional level as before. While the medical model is most typically seen within the medical profession, including among psychiatrists, the wellness model is more commonly used in the counseling profession.

35. C: In order to become a National Certified Counselor, a Master's degree in counseling is required. In addition, counselors must also have a minimum of two years of post graduate experience in the field and pass a national exam. This voluntary certification is provided by the National Board of Certified Counselors and is in addition to the counselor's state license. This board also has specialty certifications including those for mental health, school, and addictions counseling.

36. D: Best practices are the ideals of any profession. Clear best practices motivate a profession's members to strive to improve their professional performances. Other ways counseling has distinguished itself has been by developing professional organizations such as the American Counseling Association, which was founded in 1952 and currently has 18 divisions with branches throughout the country. This organization publishes newsletters and scholarly journals, which also promote advancement in the field of counseling.

37. A: Assimilation occurs when members of a minority culture adopt the culture of the majority. In the process, the values and traditions of the minority culture are lost. An individual with a physical appearance is similar to that of members of the majority culture will have an easier time assimilating. As the importance of individuality and cultural diversity becomes increasingly appreciated, assimilation is increasingly viewed as an undesirable option.

38. B: Resilience is the best term to describe the family's ability to bounce back from problems or issues. It is during times of stress and disorder that a family enters a state of dysfunction. The role of the counselor is to assist in identifying the process for the family to get back to a functional state. Things that can help a family develop resilience include good communication between members, clear role expectations, and respect for each other. Some techniques that a counselor may use to help families include communication skill building, problem solving, and education on family roles.

39. B: A criterion-referenced assessment instrument compares a score to a standard. This type of assessment may also be referred to as domain-referenced or objective-

referenced. Examples of criterion-referenced assessments can often be found in education, such as a chapter test. In a chapter test, the teacher is measuring how much material the students have learned based on some standard, often depicted in the form of 90%=A, 80%=B, etc. The purpose of a criterion-referenced test is to determine if an individual has reached a level of understanding or performance. Problems with criterion-referenced tests include determining the standard and accurate measurement of the subject being taught.

40. C: Personality is the most important factor in a good counselor. While being knowledgeable, being a good communicator, and experience are all essential, it is the counselor's intention to help, which is demonstrated in the personality, that matters the most. Counselors who understand themselves, their limitations and their strengths are apt to be more genuine and open when developing and maintaining the counseling relationship. Qualities of personality that are particularly useful include self-confidence, high levels of energy, compassion, honesty, flexibility, and creativity.

41. D: In behavioral theory, classical conditioning is the learning process that requires a stimulus and a reinforcer. This type of learning often occurs in childhood with regard to fears and phobia. A behavioral therapist views the child as a blank slate with no initial fear. If the child's mother is afraid of snakes and screams every time she sees one, the child will associate screaming with the snake. Since the mother's scream most likely invokes fear in the child, he will begin to associate that fear with snakes.

42. C: According to Erikson's stages of emotional development, a child will develop feelings of either initiative or guilt between 3½ and 6 years of age. A child given the opportunity to learn about the world through exploration, creativity and play will develop feelings of initiative and gain the necessary self-confidence to succeed in school. On the other hand, a child who is stopped from these activities through scolding or other negative means will develop feelings of guilt.

43. B: According to cognitive-behavioral therapy, children in the formal operational stage are at least 12 years old and are able to think abstractly and hypothetically. This ability to think hypothetically is an abstract process that most children in the concrete operational stage are unable to do. The concrete operational stage includes children between the ages of 8 and 12. It is during this time that the child learns to think abstractly and can use rudimentary forms of logic to problem solve. However, thinking at this stage is not fully analytical.

44. A: After an individual has been diagnosed with AIDS, the average life expectancy is one year. Symptoms of AIDS include fever, sweats, weight loss, fatigue, bruising or bleeding and skin rashes. An individual can contract the HIV virus and live with it remaining dormant for 7-8 years before being diagnosed. As a counselor, it is important to understand both the physical and emotional factors that go along with this disease. Individuals may come to counseling seeking support for living with the disease; group therapies work well with these individuals.

45. D: It is not necessarily true that abused children will abuse as adults. What is true is that some abused children will continue the cycle of abuse as adults;

however, many adults who were abused as children put an end to the cycle. Child abuse is a worldwide occurrence and takes place among the poor as well as the wealthy. It is often difficult to detect abuse in the home because family members become very good at hiding it. Abuse can be verbal, emotional, or physical.

46. A: According to Erikson's stages of development, adulthood is the stage in which an individual is faced with generativity or stagnation. It is at this developmental stage that individuals want to feel that they are making a difference in their communities and the world around them. Individuals who remain active by working, volunteering in the community, or taking care of children develop feelings of generativity. On the other hand, those individuals who do not participate in activities they feel are worthy and useful develop a sense of stagnation. A counselor who recognizes stagnant feelings will be able to suggest solutions or activities that can move the client from stagnation to generativity.

47. B: Reliability refers to an assessment's ability to yield the same results from test to test. When testing reliability, researchers use a coefficient to indicate the degree of reliability. By looking at the reliability coefficient the counselor will know how beneficial the assessment will be for his purposes and this coefficient can be use in the interpretation of results. There are three main types of reliability; test-retest, where reliability is determined by the same individual taking the same test twice; parallel forms, which uses two versions of a test; and split-half reliability, which uses halves of an assessment.

48. B: The validity of an assessment is its ability to test what it says it will test. For example, an assessment to test the level of understanding for counseling topics will not ask questions about English. The validity of an assessment will tell the counselor what the results are worth. If an assessment has high validity, the counselor can be sure that the results indicate what they are testing. The validity of an assessment instrument is developed through research and identification of factors that are or are not related to various assessments. For example, suppose an assessment states that it will measure likelihood to getting into college. In order to determine validity, those factors needed to get into college must be known and included in the assessment.

49. D: Assessment results are not used to match the client with the counselor. While this match is important, assessment results are typically used for other aspects of counseling. In order to provide clients with the best possible treatment, counselors must understand the client's specific needs. Assessments help this process and provide the counselor with important information for treatment planning. Assessments can also be used to develop goals for treatment. For example, if a child is referred to the school counselor and his assessment reveals that he is significantly behind in reading, one goal can be related to reading improvement. Finally, assessments conducted throughout the therapeutic relationship can serve as markers in progress to evaluate the effectiveness of the treatment.

50. D: David Wechsler developed intelligence tests, specifically three targeted at different age groups. The Wechsler Preschool and Primary Scale of Intelligence III was designed for children ages 2-7; the Wechsler Intelligence Scale for Children 4th Edition for ages 6-16; and the Wechsler Adult Intelligence Scale-3rd Edition for

individuals ages 16-89. These intelligences assessments are one of the most frequently administered intelligence tests in schools and include various subscales to assess verbal, cognitive, perceptional, and analytical abilities. These tests have a mean score of 10 with a standard deviation of 15, meaning that the majority of people who take this test will score 85-115.

Special Report: What Your Test Score Will Tell You About Your IQ

Did you know that most standardized tests correlate very strongly with IQ? In fact, your general intelligence is a better predictor of your success than any other factor, and most tests intentionally measure this trait to some degree to ensure that those selected by the test are truly qualified for the test's purposes.

Before we can delve into the relation between your test score and IQ, I will first have to explain what exactly is IQ. Here's the formula:

Your IQ = 100 + (Number of standard deviations below or above the average)*15

Now, let's define standard deviations by using an example. If we have 5 people with 5 different heights, then first we calculate the average. Let's say the average was 65 inches. The standard deviation is the "average distance" away from the average of each of the members. It is a direct measure of variability - if the 5 people included Jackie Chan and Shaquille O'Neal, obviously there's a lot more variability in that group than a group of 5 sisters who are all within 6 inches in height of each other. The standard deviation uses a number to characterize the average range of difference within a group.

A convenient feature of most groups is that they have a "normal" distribution- makes sense that most things would be normal, right? Without getting into a bunch of statistical mumbo-jumbo, you just need to know that if you know the average of the group and the standard deviation, you can successfully predict someone's percentile rank in the group.

Confused? Let me give you an example. If instead of 5 people's heights, we had 100 people, we could figure out their rank in height JUST by knowing the average, standard deviation, and their height. We wouldn't need to know each person's height and manually rank them, we could just predict their rank based on three numbers.

What this means is that you can take your PERCENTILE rank that is often given with your test and relate this to your RELATIVE IQ of people taking the test - that is, your IQ relative to the people taking the test. Obviously, there's no way to know your actual IQ because the people taking a standardized test are usually not very good samples of the general population- many of those with extremely low IQ's never achieve a level of success or competency necessary to complete a typical standardized test. In fact, professional psychologists who measure IQ actually have to use non-written tests that can fairly measure the IQ of those not able to complete a traditional test.

The bottom line is to not take your test score too seriously, but it is fun to compute your "relative IQ" among the people who took the test with you. I've done the calculations below. Just look up your percentile rank in the left and then you'll see your "relative IQ" for your test in the right hand column-

Percentile Rank	Your Relative IQ		Percentile Rank	Your Relative IQ
99	135		59	103
98	131		58	103
97	128		57	103
96	126		56	102
95	125		55	102
94	123		54	102
93	122		53	101
92	121		52	101
91	120		51	100
90	119		50	100
89	118		49	100
88	118		48	99
87	117		47	99
86	116		46	98
85	116		45	98
84	115		44	98
83	114		43	97
82	114		42	97
81	113		41	97
80	113		40	96
79	112		39	96
78	112		38	95
77	111		37	95
76	111		36	95
75	110		35	94
74	110		34	94
73	109		33	93
72	109		32	93
71	108		31	93
70	108		30	92
69	107		29	92
68	107		28	91
67	107		27	91
66	106		26	90
65	106		25	90
64	105		24	89
63	105		23	89
62	105		22	88
61	104		21	88
60	104		20	87

Special Report: What is Test Anxiety and How to Overcome It?

The very nature of tests caters to some level of anxiety, nervousness or tension, just as we feel for any important event that occurs in our lives. A little bit of anxiety or nervousness can be a good thing. It helps us with motivation, and makes achievement just that much sweeter. However, too much anxiety can be a problem; especially if it hinders our ability to function and perform.

"Test anxiety," is the term that refers to the emotional reactions that some test-takers experience when faced with a test or exam. Having a fear of testing and exams is based upon a rational fear, since the test-taker's performance can shape the course of an academic career. Nevertheless, experiencing excessive fear of examinations will only interfere with the test-takers ability to perform, and his/her chances to be successful.

There are a large variety of causes that can contribute to the development and sensation of test anxiety. These include, but are not limited to lack of performance and worrying about issues surrounding the test.

Lack of Preparation

Lack of preparation can be identified by the following behaviors or situations:

Not scheduling enough time to study, and therefore cramming the night before the test or exam
Managing time poorly, to create the sensation that there is not enough time to do everything
Failing to organize the text information in advance, so that the study material consists of the entire text and not simply the pertinent information
Poor overall studying habits

Worrying, on the other hand, can be related to both the test taker, or many other factors around him/her that will be affected by the results of the test. These include worrying about:

Previous performances on similar exams, or exams in general
How friends and other students are achieving
The negative consequences that will result from a poor grade or failure

There are three primary elements to test anxiety. Physical components, which involve the same typical bodily reactions as those to acute anxiety (to be discussed below). Emotional factors have to do with fear or panic. Mental or cognitive issues concerning attention spans and memory abilities.

Physical Signals

There are many different symptoms of test anxiety, and these are not limited to mental and emotional strain. Frequently there are a range of physical signals that will let a test taker know that he/she is suffering from test anxiety. These bodily changes can include the following:

Perspiring
Sweaty palms
Wet, trembling hands
Nausea
Dry mouth
A knot in the stomach
Headache
Faintness
Muscle tension
Aching shoulders, back and neck
Rapid heart beat
Feeling too hot/cold

To recognize the sensation of test anxiety, a test-taker should monitor him/herself for the following sensations:

The physical distress symptoms as listed above
Emotional sensitivity, expressing emotional feelings such as the need to cry or laugh too much, or a sensation of anger or helplessness
A decreased ability to think, causing the test-taker to blank out or have racing thoughts that are hard to organize or control.

Though most students will feel some level of anxiety when faced with a test or exam, the majority can cope with that anxiety and maintain it at a manageable level. However, those who cannot are faced with a very real and very serious condition, which can and should be controlled for the immeasurable benefit of this sufferer.

Naturally, these sensations lead to negative results for the testing experience. The most common effects of test anxiety have to do with nervousness and mental blocking.

Nervousness

Nervousness can appear in several different levels:

The test-taker's difficulty, or even inability to read and understand the questions on the test
The difficulty or inability to organize thoughts to a coherent form
The difficulty or inability to recall key words and concepts relating to the testing questions (especially essays)
The receipt of poor grades on a test, though the test material was well known by the test taker

Conversely, a person may also experience mental blocking, which involves:

Blanking out on test questions
Only remembering the correct answers to the questions when the test has already finished.

Fortunately for test anxiety sufferers, beating these feelings, to a large degree, has to do with proper preparation. When a test taker has a feeling of preparedness, then anxiety will be dramatically lessened.

The first step to resolving anxiety issues is to distinguish which of the two types of anxiety are being suffered. If the anxiety is a direct result of a lack of preparation, this should be considered a normal reaction, and the anxiety level (as opposed to the test results) shouldn't be anything to worry about. However, if, when adequately prepared, the test-taker still panics, blanks out, or seems to overreact, this is not a fully rational reaction. While this can be considered normal too, there are many ways to combat and overcome these effects.

Remember that anxiety cannot be entirely eliminated, however, there are ways to minimize it, to make the anxiety easier to manage. Preparation is one of the best ways to minimize test anxiety. Therefore the following techniques are wise in order to best fight off any anxiety that may want to build.

To begin with, try to avoid cramming before a test, whenever it is possible. By trying to memorize an entire term's worth of information in one day, you'll be shocking your system, and not giving yourself a very good chance to absorb the information. This is an easy path to anxiety, so for those who suffer from test anxiety, cramming should not even be considered an option.

Instead of cramming, work throughout the semester to combine all of the material which is presented throughout the semester, and work on it gradually as the course goes by, making sure to master the main concepts first, leaving minor details for a week or so before the test.

To study for the upcoming exam, be sure to pose questions that may be on the examination, to gauge the ability to answer them by integrating the ideas from your texts, notes and lectures, as well as any supplementary readings.

If it is truly impossible to cover all of the information that was covered in that particular term, concentrate on the most important portions, that can be covered very well. Learn these concepts as best as possible, so that when the test comes, a goal can be made to use these concepts as presentations of your knowledge.

In addition to study habits, changes in attitude are critical to beating a struggle with test anxiety. In fact, an improvement of the perspective over the entire test-taking experience can actually help a test taker to enjoy studying and therefore improve the overall experience. Be certain not to overemphasize the significance of the grade - know that the result of the test is neither a reflection of self worth, nor is it a measure of intelligence; one grade will not predict a person's future success.

To improve an overall testing outlook, the following steps should be tried:

Keeping in mind that the most reasonable expectation for taking a test is to expect to try to demonstrate as much of what you know as you possibly can.
Reminding ourselves that a test is only one test; this is not the only one, and there will be others.
The thought of thinking of oneself in an irrational, all-or-nothing term should be avoided at all costs.
A reward should be designated for after the test, so there's something to look forward to. Whether it be going to a movie, going out to eat, or simply visiting friends, schedule it in advance, and do it no matter what result is expected on the exam.

Test-takers should also keep in mind that the basics are some of the most important things, even beyond anti-anxiety techniques and studying. Never neglect the basic social, emotional and biological needs, in order to try to absorb information. In order to best achieve, these three factors must be held as just as important as the studying itself.

Study Steps

Remember the following important steps for studying:

Maintain healthy nutrition and exercise habits. Continue both your recreational activities and social pass times. These both contribute to your physical and emotional well being.
Be certain to get a good amount of sleep, especially the night before the test, because when you're overtired you are not able to perform to the best of your best ability.
Keep the studying pace to a moderate level by taking breaks when they are needed, and varying the work whenever possible, to keep the mind fresh instead of getting bored.
When enough studying has been done that all the material that can be learned has been learned, and the test taker is prepared for the test, stop studying and do something relaxing such as listening to music, watching a movie, or taking a warm bubble bath.

There are also many other techniques to minimize the uneasiness or apprehension that is experienced along with test anxiety before, during, or even after the examination. In fact, there are a great deal of things that can be done to stop anxiety from interfering with lifestyle and performance. Again, remember that anxiety will not be eliminated entirely, and it shouldn't be. Otherwise that "up" feeling for exams would not exist, and most of us depend on that sensation to perform better than usual. However, this anxiety has to be at a level that is manageable.

Of course, as we have just discussed, being prepared for the exam is half the battle right away. Attending all classes, finding out what knowledge will be expected on the exam, and knowing the exam schedules are easy steps to lowering anxiety. Keeping up with work will remove the need to cram, and efficient study habits will eliminate wasted time. Studying should be done in an ideal location for concentration, so that it is simple to become interested in the material and give it complete attention. A method such as SQ3R (Survey, Question, Read, Recite, Review) is a wonderful key to follow to make sure that the study habits are as effective as possible, especially in the case of learning from a textbook. Flashcards are great techniques for memorization. Learning to take good notes will mean that notes will be full of useful information, so that less sifting will need to be done to seek out what is pertinent for studying. Reviewing notes after class and then again on occasion will keep the information fresh in the mind. From notes that have been taken summary sheets and outlines can be made for simpler reviewing.

A study group can also be a very motivational and helpful place to study, as there will be a sharing of ideas, all of the minds can work together, to make sure that everyone understands, and the studying will be made more interesting because it will be a social occasion.

Basically, though, as long as the test-taker remains organized and self confident, with efficient study habits, less time will need to be spent studying, and higher grades will be achieved.

To become self confident, there are many useful steps. The first of these is "self talk." It has been shown through extensive research, that self-talk for students who suffer from test anxiety, should be well monitored, in order to make sure that it contributes to self confidence as opposed to sinking the student. Frequently the self talk of test-anxious students is negative or self-defeating, thinking that everyone else is smarter and faster, that they always mess up, and that if they don't do well, they'll fail the entire course. It is important to decreasing anxiety that awareness is made of self talk. Try writing any negative self thoughts and then disputing them with a positive statement instead. Begin self-encouragement as though it was a friend speaking. Repeat positive statements to help reprogram the mind to believing in successes instead of failures.

Helpful Techniques

Other extremely helpful techniques include:

Self-visualization of doing well and reaching goals
While aiming for an "A" level of understanding, don't try to "overprotect" by setting your expectations lower. This will only convince the mind to stop studying in order to meet the lower expectations.
Don't make comparisons with the results or habits of other students. These are individual factors, and different things work for different people, causing different results.
Strive to become an expert in learning what works well, and what can be done in order to improve. Consider collecting this data in a journal.
Create rewards for after studying instead of doing things before studying that will only turn into avoidance behaviors.
Make a practice of relaxing - by using methods such as progressive relaxation, self-hypnosis, guided imagery, etc - in order to make relaxation an automatic sensation.
Work on creating a state of relaxed concentration so that concentrating will take on the focus of the mind, so that none will be wasted on worrying.
Take good care of the physical self by eating well and getting enough sleep.
Plan in time for exercise and stick to this plan.

Beyond these techniques, there are other methods to be used before, during and after the test that will help the test-taker perform well in addition to overcoming anxiety.

Before the exam comes the academic preparation. This involves establishing a study schedule and beginning at least one week before the actual date of the test. By doing this, the anxiety of not having enough time to study for the test will be automatically eliminated. Moreover, this will make the studying a much more effective experience, ensuring that the learning will be an easier process. This relieves much undue pressure on the test-taker.

Summary sheets, note cards, and flash cards with the main concepts and examples of these main concepts should be prepared in advance of the actual studying time. A topic should never be eliminated from this process. By omitting a topic because it isn't expected to be on the test is only setting up the test-taker for anxiety should it actually appear on the exam. Utilize the course syllabus for laying out the topics that should be studied. Carefully go over the notes that were made in class, paying special attention to any of the issues that the professor took special care to emphasize while lecturing in class. In the textbooks, use the chapter review, or if possible, the chapter tests, to begin your review.

It may even be possible to ask the instructor what information will be covered on the exam, or what the format of the exam will be (for example, multiple choice, essay, free form, true-false). Additionally, see if it is possible to find out how many questions will be on the test. If a review sheet or sample test has been offered by the professor, make good use of it, above anything else, for the preparation for the test. Another great resource for getting to know the examination is reviewing tests from previous semesters. Use these tests to review, and aim to achieve a 100% score on each of the possible topics. With a few exceptions, the goal that you set for yourself is the highest one that you will reach.

Take all of the questions that were assigned as homework, and rework them to any other possible course material. The more problems reworked, the more skill and confidence will form as a result. When forming the solution to a problem, write out each of the steps. Don't simply do head work. By doing as many steps on paper as possible, much clarification and therefore confidence will be formed. Do this with as many homework problems as possible, before checking the answers. By checking the answer after each problem, a reinforcement will exist, that will not be on the exam. Study situations should be as exam-like as possible, to prime the test-taker's system for the experience. By waiting to check the answers at the end, a psychological advantage will be formed, to decrease the stress factor.

Another fantastic reason for not cramming is the avoidance of confusion in concepts, especially when it comes to mathematics. 8-10 hours of study will become one hundred percent more effective if it is spread out over a week or at least several days, instead of doing it all in one sitting. Recognize that the human brain requires time in order to assimilate new material, so frequent breaks and a span of study time over several days will be much more beneficial.

Additionally, don't study right up until the point of the exam. Studying should stop a minimum of one hour before the exam begins. This allows the brain to rest and put things in their proper order. This will also provide the time to become as relaxed as possible when going into the examination room. The test-taker will also have time to eat well and eat sensibly. Know that the brain needs food as much as the rest of the body. With enough food and enough sleep, as well as a relaxed attitude, the body and the mind are primed for success.

Avoid any anxious classmates who are talking about the exam. These students only spread anxiety, and are not worth sharing the anxious sentimentalities.

Before the test also involves creating a positive attitude, so mental preparation should also be a point of concentration. There are many keys to creating a positive attitude. Should fears become rushing in, make a visualization of taking the exam, doing well, and seeing an A written on the paper. Write out a list of affirmations that will bring a feeling of confidence, such as "I am doing well in my English class," "I studied well and know my material," "I enjoy this class." Even if the affirmations aren't believed at first, it sends a positive message to the subconscious which will result in an alteration of the overall belief system, which is the system that creates reality.

If a sensation of panic begins, work with the fear and imagine the very worst! Work through the entire scenario of not passing the test, failing the entire course, and dropping out of school, followed by not getting a job, and pushing a shopping cart through the dark alley where you'll live. This will place things into perspective! Then, practice deep breathing and create a visualization of the opposite situation - achieving an "A" on the exam, passing the entire course, receiving the degree at a graduation ceremony.

On the day of the test, there are many things to be done to ensure the best results, as well as the most calm outlook. The following stages are suggested in order to maximize test-taking potential:

Begin the examination day with a moderate breakfast, and avoid any coffee or beverages with caffeine if the test taker is prone to jitters. Even people who are used to managing caffeine can feel jittery or light-headed when it is taken on a test day.
Attempt to do something that is relaxing before the examination begins. As last minute cramming clouds the mastering of overall concepts, it is better to use this time to create a calming outlook.
Be certain to arrive at the test location well in advance, in order to provide time to select a location that is away from doors, windows and other distractions, as well as giving enough time to relax before the test begins.
Keep away from anxiety generating classmates who will upset the sensation of stability and relaxation that is being attempted before the exam.
Should the waiting period before the exam begins cause anxiety, create a self-distraction by reading a light magazine or something else that is relaxing and simple.

During the exam itself, read the entire exam from beginning to end, and find out how much time should be allotted to each individual problem. Once writing the exam, should more time be taken for a problem, it should be abandoned, in order to begin another problem. If there is time at the end, the unfinished problem can always be returned to and completed.

Read the instructions very carefully - twice - so that unpleasant surprises won't follow during or after the exam has ended.

When writing the exam, pretend that the situation is actually simply the completion of homework within a library, or at home. This will assist in forming a relaxed atmosphere, and will allow the brain extra focus for the complex thinking function.

Begin the exam with all of the questions with which the most confidence is felt. This will build the confidence level regarding the entire exam and will begin a quality momentum. This will also create encouragement for trying the problems where uncertainty resides.

Going with the "gut instinct" is always the way to go when solving a problem. Second guessing should be avoided at all costs. Have confidence in the ability to do well.

For essay questions, create an outline in advance that will keep the mind organized and make certain that all of the points are remembered. For multiple choice, read every answer, even if the correct one has been spotted - a better one may exist.

Continue at a pace that is reasonable and not rushed, in order to be able to work carefully. Provide enough time to go over the answers at the end, to check for small errors that can be corrected.

Should a feeling of panic begin, breathe deeply, and think of the feeling of the body releasing sand through its pores. Visualize a calm, peaceful place, and include all of the sights, sounds and sensations of this image. Continue the deep breathing, and take a few minutes to continue this with closed eyes. When all is well again, return to the test.

If a "blanking" occurs for a certain question, skip it and move on to the next question. There will be time to return to the other question later. Get everything done that can be done, first, to guarantee all the grades that can be compiled, and to build all of the confidence possible. Then return to the weaker questions to build the marks from there.

Remember, one's own reality can be created, so as long as the belief is there, success will follow. And remember: anxiety can happen later, right now, there's an exam to be written!

After the examination is complete, whether there is a feeling for a good grade or a bad grade, don't dwell on the exam, and be certain to follow through on the reward that was promised…and enjoy it! Don't dwell on any mistakes that have been made, as there is nothing that can be done at this point anyway.

Additionally, don't begin to study for the next test right away. Do something relaxing for a while, and let the mind relax and prepare itself to begin absorbing information again.

From the results of the exam - both the grade and the entire experience, be certain to learn from what has gone on. Perfect studying habits and work some more on confidence in order to make the next examination experience even better than the last one.

Learn to avoid places where openings occurred for laziness, procrastination and day dreaming.

Use the time between this exam and the next one to better learn to relax, even learning to relax on cue, so that any anxiety can be controlled during the next exam. Learn how to relax the body. Slouch in your chair if that helps. Tighten and then relax all of the different muscle groups, one group at a time, beginning with the feet and then working all the way up to the neck and face. This will ultimately relax the muscles more than they were to begin with. Learn how to breathe deeply and comfortably, and focus on this breathing going in and out as a relaxing thought. With every exhale, repeat the word "relax."

As common as test anxiety is, it is very possible to overcome it. Make yourself one of the test-takers who overcome this frustrating hindrance.

Special Report: Retaking the Test: What Are Your Chances at Improving Your Score?

After going through the experience of taking a major test, many test takers feel that once is enough. The test usually comes during a period of transition in the test taker's life, and taking the test is only one of a series of important events. With so many distractions and conflicting recommendations, it may be difficult for a test taker to rationally determine whether or not he should retake the test after viewing his scores.

The importance of the test usually only adds to the burden of the retake decision. However, don't be swayed by emotion. There a few simple questions that you can ask yourself to guide you as you try to determine whether a retake would improve your score:

1. What went wrong? Why wasn't your score what you expected?

Can you point to a single factor or problem that you feel caused the low score? Were you sick on test day? Was there an emotional upheaval in your life that caused a distraction? Were you late for the test or not able to use the full time allotment? If you can point to any of these specific, individual problems, then a retake should definitely be considered.

2. Is there enough time to improve?

Many problems that may show up in your score report may take a lot of time for improvement. A deficiency in a particular math skill may require weeks or months of tutoring and studying to improve. If you have enough time to improve an identified weakness, then a retake should definitely be considered.

3. How will additional scores be used? Will a score average, highest score, or most recent score be used?

Different test scores may be handled completely differently. If you've taken the test multiple times, sometimes your highest score is used, sometimes your average score is computed and used, and sometimes your most recent score is used. Make sure you understand what method will be used to evaluate your scores, and use that to help you determine whether a retake should be considered.

4. Are my practice test scores significantly higher than my actual test score?

If you have taken a lot of practice tests and are consistently scoring at a much higher level than your actual test score, then you should consider a retake. However, if you've taken five practice tests and only one of your scores was higher than your actual test score, or if your practice test scores were only slightly higher than your actual test score, then it is unlikely that you will significantly increase your score.

5. Do I need perfect scores or will I be able to live with this score? Will this score still allow me to follow my dreams?

What kind of score is acceptable to you? Is your current score "good enough?" Do you have to have a certain score in order to pursue the future of your dreams? If you won't be happy with your current score, and there's no way that you could live with it, then you should consider a retake. However, don't get your hopes up. If you are looking for significant improvement, that may or may not be possible. But if you won't be happy otherwise, it is at least worth the effort.
Remember that there are other considerations. To achieve your dream, it is likely that your grades may also be taken into account. A great test score is usually not the only thing necessary to succeed. Make sure that you aren't overemphasizing the importance of a high test score.

Furthermore, a retake does not always result in a higher score. Some test takers will score lower on a retake, rather than higher. One study shows that one-fourth of test takers will achieve a significant improvement in test score, while one-sixth of test takers will actually show a decrease. While this shows that most test takers will improve, the majority will only improve their scores a little and a retake may not be worth the test taker's effort.

Finally, if a test is taken only once and is considered in the added context of good grades on the part of a test taker, the person reviewing the grades and scores may be tempted to assume that the test taker just had a bad day while taking the test, and may discount the low test score in favor of the high grades. But if the test is retaken and the scores are approximately the same, then the validity of the low scores are only confirmed. Therefore, a retake could actually hurt a test taker by definitely bracketing a test taker's score ability to a limited range.